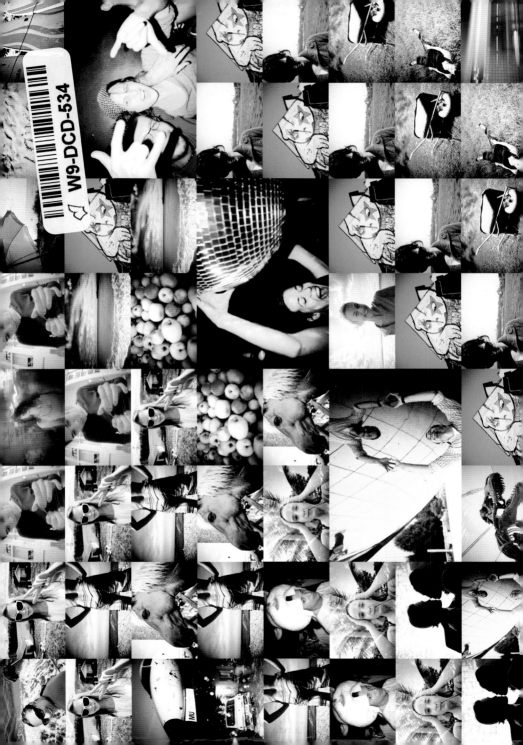

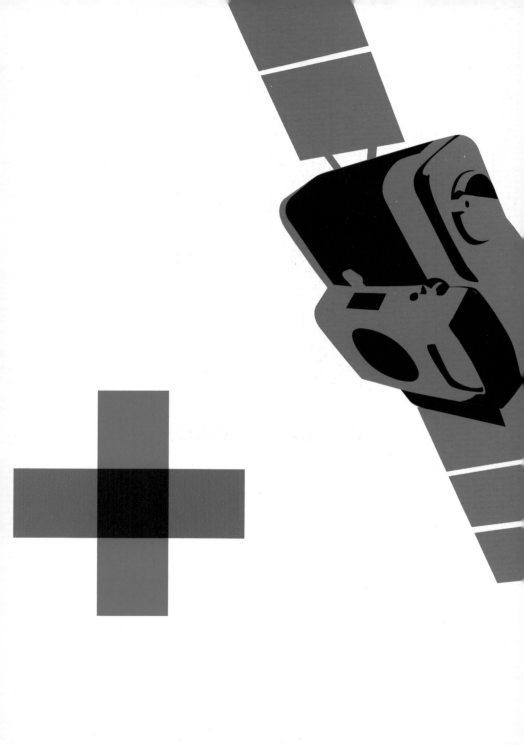

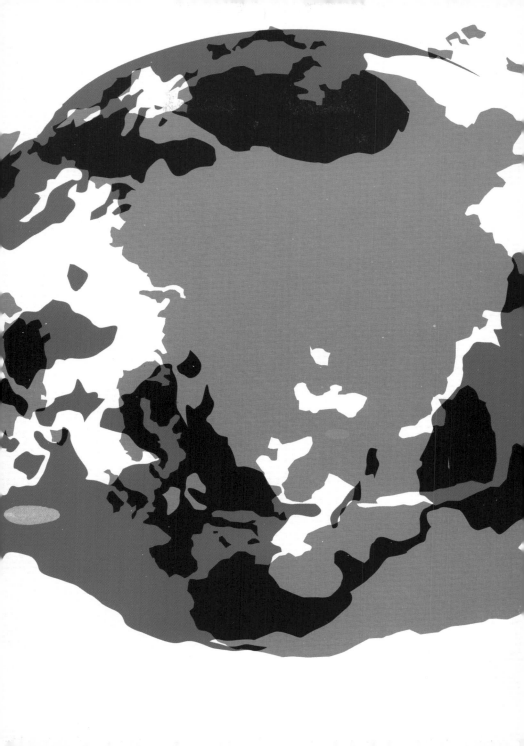

образцу.
9. *Размер после покр...

1. Pressure die casting PTM 3-443-73
2. Casting radii ~ max 0,3 mm
3. Unspecified limit dimensional deviations – ±0,1 mm
4. On surface "Д" traces of ejectors buried for max. 0,2
5. On surface "М" trace of removed gate not protruding allowed
6. Letter "Т" to be filled with temper polyvinylacetate d...
   titanium white...

"If you want to build a ship, don't drum up people to collect wood and don't assign them tasks and work, but rather teach them to long for the endless immensity of the sea."

Antoine de Saint-Exupéry

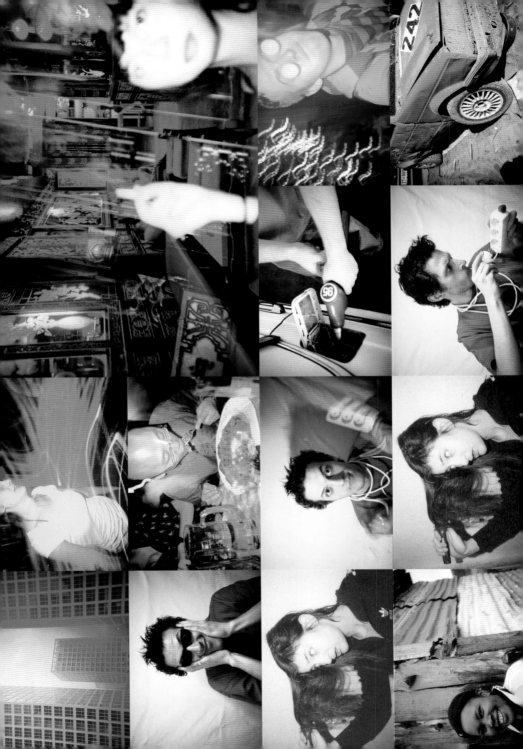

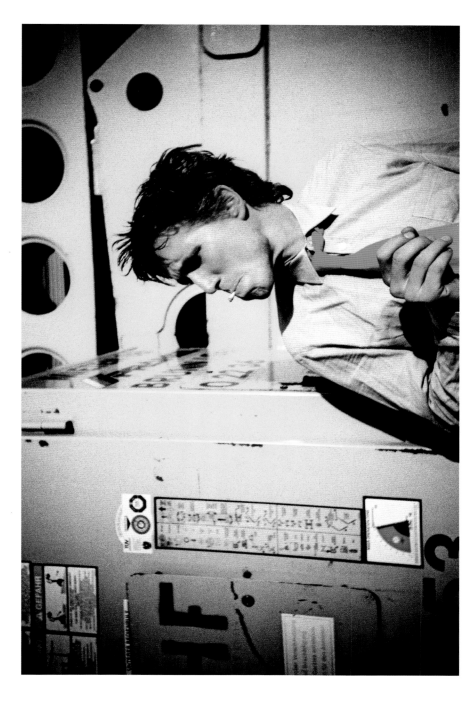

COLD DRINKS
SUPER SOFT ICE
HOT DOGS
HOT DOGS
MINERAL WATER
ICE CREAMS
Coca-Cola
TAHIR

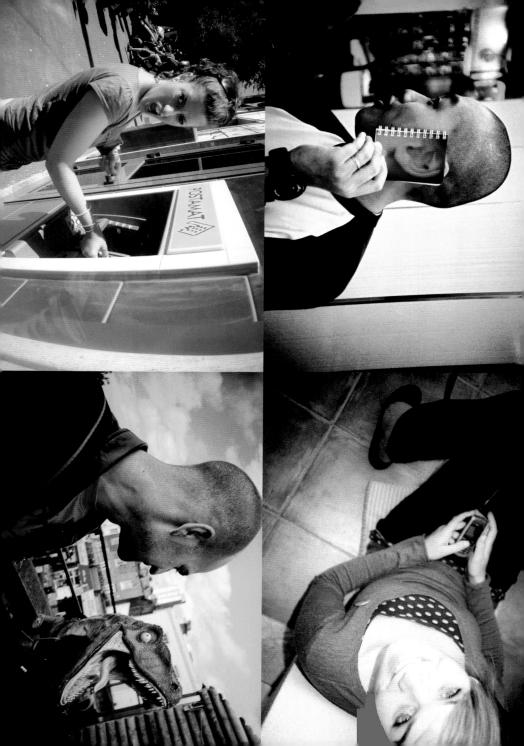

CONTENTS >>

THE 10 GOLDEN RULES OF LOMOGRAPHY

At the very core of Lomography lie the 10 Golden Rules. Memorise them, recite them by heart, or break all the rules; whichever way, be ready to throw all your inhibitions about photography to the wind.

TAKE YOUR CAMERA EVERYWHERE YOU GO. Lomography Golden Rule No. 1

Like any passion, you can never plan or predict Lomography. It's like your inner voice and your deepest desire working at the same time. Lomography is waiting around the corner to say "Hey good looking, wanna go for a ride?"

You might be at a garage, in the woods, on an Airbus or in a saloon, in the Hammam, at work, at a boulangerie or on the Fujiyama, at dinner with King Charles or in bed with breakfast, and suddenly it strikes you.

Your hands (your trigger finger!) start trembling, your eyes become hungry, your soul is burning for images, images, images and you grab your LOMO LC-A, click, ahhhhhhh, click, click, click, now it's better, and another click, it happens and it's real; the unstoppable Lomographic desire to document your surroundings is overwhelming you and will never let go.

And nor will you: you're feeling Lomography, you're pulling out the LOMO LC-A and life starts pulsating. It's the best addiction in the world. Did you know that the best photos come out of spontaneous, extreme and impulsive situations and that many of them are therefore never taken, simply due to the lack of a camera? Your LOMO LC-A however is so compact and fast that it becomes an integral part of your body and soul. Hence, it touches photographic spheres that other cameras hardly come close to: the unexpected, spontaneous and sudden moments; the most vibrant sides of life! Therefore: open your eyes and have your LOMO LC-A always and everywhere with you.

USE IT ANY TIME – DAY AND NIGHT.
Lomography Golden Rule No. 2

Every second is special for you and your LOMO LC-A; every moment is monumental! When you are Lomographing, you're not only living your life at the present with more intensity and excitement, but you're also conserving the present for your future.

All is possible with the help of your bright, dark, moody, blurred, sharp, colourful, grey, indefinable, straightforward, romantic and fully packed Lomographs! Your feelings, your memory and your Lomographs; they all mix up to a new, complete, more authentic view and perception of yourself and your life. You don't only exist in sunshine, daytime, on holidays and on Aunt Frida's birthday, do you?

So keep shooting in any environment, every day and every night, be aware, and create yourself, your being, your design. Shoot relentlessly and give your memory a kick in the arse with your lovely, crap, beautiful, artistic and silly Lomographs. Esse est percipi est Lomographi. Use your LOMO LC-A whenever you're alive!

LOMOGRAPHY IS NOT AN INTERFERENCE IN YOUR LIFE, BUT PART OF IT.

There's no chance of relationship phobia: the LOMO LC-A is what you've always wanted in life; your new best friend, drinking buddy, spiritual leader and lover all at the same time.

You work with the camera, you drink with the camera, you sleep with the camera. Lomography becomes a natural and communicative habit of your life, just like talking, walking, eating, thinking, laughing and loving. As a Lomographer, you are not only photographing a situation, you are an essential part of the situation itself. Life inhales Lomography and Lomography inhales life.

You laugh and you Lomograph, you cry and you Lomograph, you walk and you Lomograph, you talk and you Lomograph, you think and you Lomograph, you love and you Lomograph and you Lomograph and you Lomograph. Lomography is a powerful sign of your existence, a constant confession of your lust for life and a magnetic field of your most intense feelings.

TRY THE SHOT FROM THE HIP.
Lomography Golden Rule No. 4

A normal photographer's point of view – looking through the view-finder – is somehow always physically finite; it's limited to somewhere between 1.1 metres and 2.2 metres above ground. But what happens down below and up above, from a dog, cat, baby, bug, slug, bird and insect perspective?

Don't hide behind your camera; break free from nonsensical conventions. Don't look through the viewfinder; forget about safety margins and unnecessary shyness! Hands up, hands down, hands forward, Lomograph from up to down and down to up, from the front to you and from you to nowhere, shoes, socks, toes, hips, buttons, belts, butts; aloha! Your LOMO LC-A is as handy as a glove and equips you with deadly fast zone-focusing abilities that let you capture a situation in a split second. Try the shot from the hip to experience absolutely free and boundless dimensions of sight!

APPROACH THE OBJECTS OF YOUR LOMOGRAPHIC DESIRE AS CLOSE AS POSSIBLE. Lomography Golden Rule No. 5

An essential part of your Lomographic existence is to get right to the bottom of things and investigate the world from the inside. Just as with people, you have to be sweet, nice, comprehensive and interested to get to know the very inside of your subject.

As soon as you feel the right moment – take a picture! Try it and you'll see that the deep affection for your Lomographed subject is strongly reflected in your image. Get in contact with your subject and build up a relationship. Smile, hello hello, the LOMO LC-A is part and mediator of your relationship, good morning, click, the camera helps you to get to know your motives and is, after all, a good reason to talk to

someone at boring parties. Click click, that's gonna be a nice picture, click, can I send it to you by email?, click, wonderful, click, I love you, click, communicate, talk! More communication equals better Lomography; Get close, even closer, don't be afraid: laugh and everyone will not only love you and your LOMO LC-A but will also realise that Lomography is the most natural thing on earth!

DON'T THINK. [WILLIAM FIREBRACE]
Lomography Golden Rule No. 6

Your brightest and clearest insights are always your very first impressions. They happen between moments of sensual, visual perception where information is delivered from your senses to your brain and remains unfiltered.

Milliseconds later it's already too late: your big, clumsy, party-pooping melancholic reasoning has put an end to the fun and divided your former beautifully pure perception into boring concepts, abstractions, ideas and problems. That's life, sorry... Not! We found a wonderful and easy way to get rid of this convention: Don't think!

Throw your intellectual socialisation over board, let the unfiltered flow of information circulate freely, untreated and unrated in your mind. Shoot, feel, perceive and shoot, have fun, shoot whatever catches your eye, whatever attracts you, astounds you, excites you, seduces you. Lomography is a surprising diversion to your egghead-life and will enlighten you with true, simple and wonderful revelations.

BE FAST . Lomography Golden Rule No. 7

Our world moves like a high-speed train without brakes and is entangled in ultra-complex systems that most people, in fact all of us, just don't understand anymore – how exciting for the Lomographic eye!

Movements, actions and Lomographic moments are not reading the paper and waiting for you to take pictures of them... the pool attendant with the big belly, the dance champion with the tight dress, the dog with the pink tie, the bus driver with the fat glasses, your dad in the shower. Believe us; they are not crazy about you taking pictures of them – but you certainly are!

So, cowgirls and cowboys: calmly hold your finger towards your LOMO LC-A's zone focusing meter; trust in yourself and in the automatic exposure, grab your guts and be quick to catch the wink of time and accidental destiny. Hold your breath, be brave, take a chance, move, shoot, run, have fun, act fast – that's Lomography!

YOU DON'T HAVE TO KNOW BEFORE-HAND WHAT YOU CAPTURED ON FILM.

Lomography Golden Rule No. 8

You can never foresee what you're getting with the LOMO LC-A, as you find yourself in constant interaction between Russo-Chinese mechanics, raw (and quite often expired) film, chemical emulsion baths, the goodwill of your lab technician, natural and artificial light, your artistic guidance and many other factors that can't be relied on. Moreover, Lomography is often an unconscious act that can't be controlled at all.

Lomographs always emerge from a plethora of different and unexpected situations, ideas, views and intentions. It's always up to you. Your subtle play with the outside world and its related coincidences make the choice- to Lomograph or not to Lomograph?

You do it because it's great fun, because it makes you curious, because it's very exciting to know that you never know what you'll get and because it allows your creativity, intuition and inspiration to soar heights you never imagined! Living with the LOMO LC-A means always living with unpredictability, uncertainty and coincidence; it is therefore living in freedom.

AFTERWARDS EITHER.

A few days later you get your Lomographs from the lab and can't believe your eyes: who's that? What's that colour? When did I shoot that?

Whose hair is this? Is that you? No it's Sabrina... interesting, and Hansi's feet too... bewildering, your butterfly collection, what a shame, a bottle of schnapps, a huge head, blurs, surprises, smiles, teeth, accidental double-exposures... Oh well, you'll never completely understand the world. But you'll understand your Lomographs even less! Don't try to analyse them: look at them in a different way and let them tell you their story, which is also automatically your story.

Your Lomographic actions are a constant record of your existence that illustrates the adventures of your life in all its anomalies, moods, shapes, colours, faces and blurs. You don't need to know afterwards what's on your film – just read between the lines, between the Lomographs, learn to read their forms, feelings, expressions, their swings, their grooves: your life!

DON'T WORRY ABOUT ANY RULES.
Lomography Golden Rule No. 10

Don't listen to others; remain true to yourself, follow your inner Lomographic voice and never forget that not all that glitters is a golden rule. Discover your own Lomography, forget about your education, socialisation, indoctrination, knowledge and everything you've learnt and not learnt about photography.

Set free your innermost desires, never stop moving, never stop Lomographing; believe in yourself, focus on the important and not so important things, enjoy life in all its variations, forget about the camera in your hand and shoot 'til your eyes are glowing!

WHAT THE HELL IS LOMOGRAPHY?

Lomography

was founded due to a series of happy coincidences. It all started with the newly opened borders to the East in 1991. There was a renewed freshness in the air making that charming "click" of the LOMO oh so attractive to us. At that moment in time our excitement for the tiny Russian camera could hardly be contained...

The Lomographer and The Lomographic Community

We then put this approach into practice in the most impossible of situations imaginable, from the most impossible positions imaginable, only then to print them as cheaply as imaginable! The results are blurry, colourful, vivid and authentic analogue photographs that reflect a direct, sensitive, barefaced and genuine impression of your adventures on this beautiful planet. Anyway, less talk more action! As soon as you take the LOMO LC-A out and have absorbed the 10 Golden Rules, you will quickly begin to understand Lomography through your own thoughts and feelings.

The LOMO LC-A's unconventional way of taking pictures, coupled with the cheap price of film development in Austria (a cheapo supermarket chain made it four times cheaper than before!) has made Lomography what it is today. Our approach: taking as many analogue-film photographs or Lomographs rather, as possible, always and everywhere.

Reading this little book could very likely mean that you have already purchased a LOMO LC-A camera. If this is the case, then that is great news for you as it automatically makes you a member of the Lomographic Society. However, if you don't own a LOMO LC-A, then you too are heartily invited to read on (and get a camera as soon as you've finished reading). At the moment, we boast more than 500,000 active members across the world that share the idea of Lomography as an interactive, democratic, creative, social, artistic, cultural, (some might say) crazy philosophy and way of life.

This community of Lomographers has always been the core of Lomography. Who are the Lomographers? Most of them are everyday artists who like to take photos relentlessly and store, share and contribute their images in off-, as well as, online communities. Whether alone or in groups, they roam through their environment (cities, landscapes, woods, space, time) shooting whatever catches their ever-attentive eye, sharing their results with like-minded people whenever possible.

Most of the Lomographers [1] store their photos as prints in their shoeboxes and as digitally scanned images in their LomoHomes. Many of them [2] share their photos via their online portfolios, at homemade exhibitions, on LomoWalls (read more about this later), in art forums, clubs, shops, public places, squares, temples and the like. Finally, a lot of Lomographers [3] contribute to worldwide competitions where their pictures are used for international collaborations, book projects and sometimes giant exhibitions showing hundreds of thousands of images at a time.

Our approach: taking as many photographs as possible in the most impossible of situations possible and from the most impossible positions possible.

Lomographic Products & Tools

When we started shooting with the LOMO LC-A in 1991, our trigger happy hands were full. A few years later however, we realised that there were many more exciting analogue cameras, tools and ideas in the world that were also tempting to the unquenchable Lomographic hunger.

That's why we searched, found, discovered and developed a plethora of cameras and accessories. These range from classic (plastic) Lomographic cameras to premium photographic gear; from pinhole cams to lenses and optics, from flashes and cable-releases to accessories, such as Lomographic bags and fashion. Following the release of the 4-lens Actionsampler in 1998, we currently feature cameras like the Supersampler, Colorsplash, Fisheye,Lomolitos, Pop 9, Oktomat, Frogeye, Horizon, Holga, Diana F+ and Diana Mini.

Quite simply; we celebrate everything related to 21st century analogue photography. But instead of telling you all about it, why not check out our most celebrated items on page 364 of this tome? In summary it may be said that we are constantly working on new cameras, accessories, books, bags, fashion, tips, tricks, newsletters, Lomographic applications, cutting-edge competitions and many other ways to serve our never-ending quest for more exciting images.

Lomography's Online Platform
www.lomography.com

Lomography.com is the place to inspire and indulge your curiosity for analogue photography and lifestyle. There's a lot going on – but you can keep up by making the most of our site's features. Leave comments, upload and share your photos, interact with other Lomographers and win some neat stuff by entering our competitions.

With a limitless amount of web space, you are able to create your own LomoHome (www.lomography.com/homes) where you upload your photos, store them and, best of all, share them with the rest of the Lomographic community. Each day one LomoHome receives the 'Lomography Home of the Day' award, that comes with a fat Piggy Point bonus (worth 1 EUR/USD each) for you to spend in the Lomography online shop.

If you contribute to the Magazine in those ways (through competitions, reviews, tips, stories, locations etc.), it's very likely that you'll make a fortune out of Piggy Points that grant you a steady discount off Lomography products.

You can check out and purchase our entire range in the Online Shop (http:// shop.lomography.com), where new stuff is constantly being added to our exciting selection of cameras, films, creative accessories and fashion. We offer you both the newest in analogue photography as well as classic deadstock cameras, professional film, expired film, infrared rolls and our very own Lomography emulsions.

Go to lomography.com immediately and see what we are talking about! The website is available in many different languages too, and allows you to customise your very own home profile to suit your personal likes and needs.

As soon as your images are uploaded on our servers, you can do almost anything with them: submit them to weekly and monthly missions and rumbles or illustrate your camera tips and tricks.

You can even contribute to our worldwide archive of Lomo-Locations (featuring the most exciting and photogenic places in the world at www.lomography.com/locations) and take part in worldwide photo competitions, which could result in having your image published or exhibited around the globe. This incredible mass of daily uploaded madness can be seen in the Photos section (www.lomography.com/photos), which is most likely the biggest database of analogue photos taken in all corners of the world.

This unbelievable stream of photos is complemented by the interactive blog called Magazine (www.lomogra-phy.com/magazine). This is your one-stop hub for analogue photography and news where everything concerning Lomography around the world (events, competitions, exhibitions, projects) can be found.

National and Worldwide Projects

In addition to its virtual romping ground, Lomography first and foremost happens in the real world, the here and now. As a globally active organisation dedicated to experimental and creative snapshot photography, we are committed to being active in the worldwide art community; as well as getting involved in non-profit projects and regularly teaming up with other international groups. When getting stuck in to such projects, we strive constantly to evoke the iconic Lomographic imagery in new and refreshing ways.

Such events and collaborations have opened the door to the established art scene and led Lomography to collaborate with institutions like the Kunsthalle Vienna; the Tokyo Metropolitan Museum of Photography; the New York Rooftop Gallery; the Museum of Modern Art, New York; Paris Photo at the Louvre; the Centre Pompidou; the Southbank Centre, London; Photokina, Cologne; and many other museums, galleries and design shops big and small. As a result we've built some spectacular Lomowalls in some of the world's most renowned locations.

We have discovered that Lomography is a great tool for connecting people and we are always working to discover ways of supporting charity projects of all kinds, in all parts of the world with Lomography's special qualities. Be it the kids of São Paolo or pupils from the Dominican Republic, homeless people in Innsbruck, Austria, a LomoWorkshop in a Serbian slum or offering support to an eye clinic in Kikuyu, Kenya. If you have an idea of using Lomography in order to help people, please contact us!

On the side of international LomoProjects we've teamed up with Absolut, Eastpak, Ripcurl, Urban Outfitters, Heineken, The White Stripes, flickr, San Miguel and BMW among others. Generally, we cooperate on photo competitions where we appeal to the creativity of Lomographers worldwide in order to collect as many exciting Lomographs as possible on a certain theme. These projects usually result in international exhibitions, books, interactive web features and the like.

You should definitely take part when we launch the next big project. Your photos could appear in a major Lomography show, which have previously been held in Moscow, New York, Vienna, Berlin, St Petersburg, Seoul, Havana, Zurich, Cologne, Madrid, Cairo, Frankfurt, Dubai, Oslo, Tokyo, Hong Kong, Singapore, Buenos Aires, Beijing, London and Bangkok. Many of these took place in public spaces such as Trafalgar Square (London), Atocha train station (Madrid), Times Square (Hong Kong) and in the subways of Vienna, São Paolo, Taipeh and Hong Kong.

The Lomography Ambassador System

All these projects and exhibitions done in cooperation would surely not have been possible without the well-proven Lomography Ambassador system. The so-called LAMB system was initially created when we received global demands from Lomographers. Here is just one example from 1995, "Hi, we're Stefan and Elisabeth from Berlin and we like Lomography. What can we do to make it happen here?"

Clearly, we needed a worldwide system for all the enthusiastic Lomographers out there who were thirsty for a platform in which they could organise, communicate and promote Lomography in their respective countries and cities. So voilà: out of the blue, at a Sunday afternoon sauna session, the Lomography ambassador system came to be. And it worked out swimmingly! Specially inaugurated Lomography Ambassadors (who usually also work as distributors of Lomographic products) now look after the community on a regional basis, putting all sorts of activities into the works such as exhibitions, parties, shows, Lomographic shootings and tours, publications and international and local art projects. They also collaborate on film, music and new media projects as well as providing local support for annual worldwide events and competitions.

Lomography Gallery Stores and Lomography Embassy Stores

Like flowers in spring more and more Lomography Gallery Stores and Embassy Stores flourish around the world. Their smell is sweet, their inside rich and prosperous and each of these stores is happy to welcome Lomographers from all over the place.

Simply put, Lomography Gallery Stores serve as a place for all your Lomographic needs, operating as a shop, gallery, workshop location, and a place to hangout at the same time. These stores are the official flagships of Lomography around the world – be sure to check them out regularly to see what's new as well as to stop by for some exclusive special editions or challenges that can't be found anywhere else.

Lomography Embassy Stores work in a similar manner yet they are mostly smaller, locally designed shops operated by the local LomoAmbassador. The worldwide network of LomoAmbassadors consists of Lomographers who represent Lomography in their respective countries who regularly organise events, challenges and competitions to keep your eyes glowing. You can expect a steady flow of such enlightening entertainment in both Embassy and Gallery Stores in your neighbourhood.

At the moment we are operating more than 20 Lomography Gallery & Embassy Stores around the world. Check the map on page 99 for their exact locations and be ready for new stores being inaugurated almost every second around the world.

Lomography Gallery Store New York (this page) and London (on the right)

Lomography Stores Worldwide

Gallery Stores

- New York
- Los Angeles
- Paris
- Berlin
- London
- Tokyo
- Seoul
- Hong Kong
- Shanghai
- Beijing
- Guangzhou
- Rio de Janeiro
- Toronto
- Milano
- Taipeh

Embassy Stores

- Bangkok
- Taichung
- Jakarta
- Sydney
- Madrid Argensola
- Madrid Echegaray
- Barcelona
- Lisbon
- Porto
- Santiago de Chile

For an up-to-date directory of all worldwide checkpoints including their addresses see: www.lomography.com/about/worldwide

The Lomographic Society International

And where is the busy hive of all this business? The centre of Lomography is situated in Vienna, Austria. We Lomographers have a nice little HQ here where all the new plans, concepts, ideas and whatnot are cooked up. Just take a moment to imagine departments dedicated to product development, graphic design, architecture, community and artistic projects, plus a web jungle – all working hard to bring you new analogue joy. Here we also house the Lomo-WorldArchive, the publishing department, the sales team, the mighty Lomographic warehouse, customer service, logistics, the accountants and some other busy folks. Basically we like coffee, classical music, strudel and Lomography.

But wait, there are many other official offices and departments as well. To be able to serve Lomographers worldwide we have offices in New York, Tokyo, Hong Kong, Seoul, Paris, Los Angeles, London, Rio de Janeiro, Bangkok and Guangzhou. These guys mostly work on product development, graphics, community and artistic projects, web design and applications, as well as sales and distribution.

We are always keen to discover something new that gives a kick to our hungry eyes and so we are constantly developing, thinking, shooting, drawing, communicating, designing, testing, writing, copying, faxing, printing, packing, pasting, sticking and so on and so forth. In fact, because we are so widespread, we don't like to think that there is a real Lomography HQ. It's always happening somewhere south or north of the equator, in fibreglass cables, cyberspace, online surveys, shout-boxes, blogs, and in Lomographers' minds worldwide. Wherever and whenever a good idea arises by accident, coincidence or wit, we grab it.

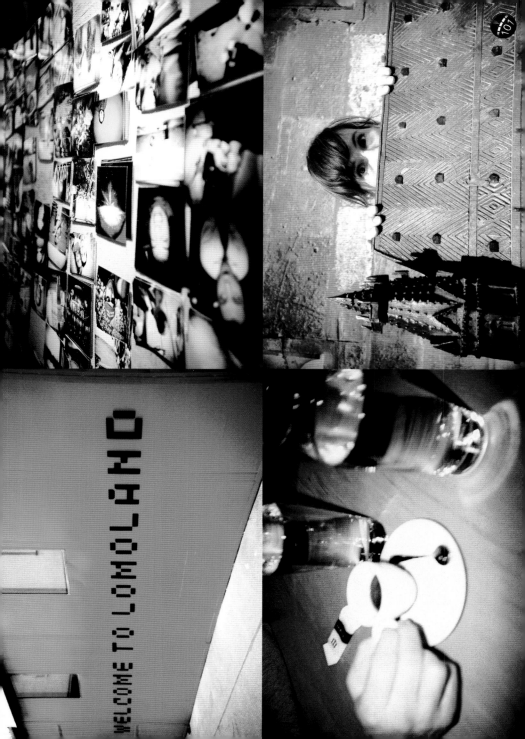

THE LOMOGRAPHIC MISSION

The Lomography Global Event

is the biggest Lomographic project of the future. This mission stands above all other activities and is the Lomographic utopia: we want to create the most extensive, diverse, colourful, authentic and spectacular snapshot portrait of our world.

The Lomography Global Event

It all began at the first Lomography World Congress in Madrid in 1997. This is where we first announced our utopian Lomographic dream of creating the biggest, all-embracing, most diverse, colourful, authentic and spectacular Lomographic portrait of the surface of the world. Since then innumerable projects in all parts of the world have followed, bringing us ever closer to this ultimate vision. Nearly one million Lomographers have participated in the creation of what has come to be the LomoWorldArchive with millions of pictures added to date.

Lomographers everywhere answered the call to ransack their secret archives, to get back out there in all ardency and work that trigger-finger to turn their very best shots into LomoWalls. The culmination of this was the biggest exhibition in Lomographic history: the LomoWorldWall in London, which exhibited 100,000 snapshots on a 250 metre-long LomoWall stretching across more than 600 square metres of Trafalgar Square. "Not bad" we thought. But ho! The mission goes on...

A DREAM OF MANKIND FOR DECADES, WE BELIEVE THAT THE PHOTO-GRAPHIC REPRESENTATION OF OUR PLANET IS NO LONGER A FANTASY.

The LomoWorldMap

The next phase in the Lomography Global Event is the LomoWorldMap. This massive project intends to create an authentic on- and offline (that is, existing in the actual, physical world) map of our planet, in all its glory, by documenting its every nook and cranny with Lomographic pictures. A dream of mankind for decades, we believe that the photographic representation of our planet is no longer a fantasy. Through the means of modern communication and the unwearied force of the worldwide Lomographic community, the LomoWorldMap can and will be realised!

This sounds like an insane event, but in reality it is quite simple and logical. We believe that with a little organisation and a can-do attitude, the whole community's snapshots can be put together to create the LomoWorldMap. Every one of us has the opportunity to become a participant and officially take care of one part of the world. This can be the whole island of Papua New Guinea (if that is what you feel like) or simply your neighbourhood, the place in which you live, or a region you feel attached to. In any case, your job as a delegate is to shoot your area like mad, collect as many images as possible (from whoever took photographs in this region in the past 150 years) and feed your discoveries to the ever-hungry LomoWorldMap. The result will be a rapidly growing, never before seen snapshot portrait of our world created by us, the Lomographers!

You should absolutely take part in our mission and participate now. Parts of the LomoWorldMap will be exhibited in places around the world so don't hesitate to load your camera immediately.

Go to www.lomography.com/lomoworldmap to take part in this adventure!

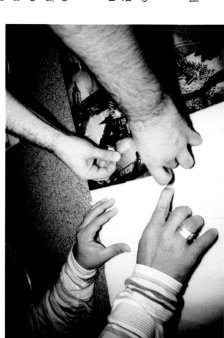

The LomoWorldArchive

We are busy beavering away with hundreds of thousands, soon to be millions of Lomographs, and the perpetual Lomographic Sisyphus project: The Lomography World Archive. These archives seek to document the planet around us in a never-ending stream. This is a visual diary by various individuals from different cultures, that is immensely big, endlessly persistent and ever-growing with ongoing portraits of the planet. This is the most comprehensive archive of the planet. A collection of millions of the artistic snapshots of all time. A collection of millions of the wackiest, most exciting and most impossible little sights and moments of our time! Approximately 1 million prints (!) are stored in our Archive in Vienna and more than 5 million pictures are stored and uploaded by worldwide Lomographers on lomography.com and its partner sites.

Furthermore, another 10 million pictures are stored in the global settlements, offices and embassies of Lomography. But the biggest archives of snapshots are to be found in the Lomographers' homes where at least 1 billion pictures are stored in shelves, under beds and in shoe-boxes… But should these images collect dust in all these boxes around the world?

No! Take a deep breath and share your pictures with us! Upload them onto our servers and show them to the whole world! Via the online photos section and LomoLocations contributing, searching, commenting and tagging photos is easier than ever before.

Are you asking what the use of all this is? Firstly, sharing the pictures we take of our planet (and sharing generally) is a great thing to do. It makes us realise day by day how beautiful the world and taking pictures of it is. Secondly, concentrating as many Lomographs as possible in one place and on one platform (lomography.com) lets us organise our photos better and makes them more accessible. This consequently leads to the third reason, the realisation of the biggest snapshot portrait of the world – the great Lomographic vision. Yes, we need you and your Lomographs! They will find it very cosy and accommodating to be amongst thousands and millions of other Lomographs and to be, with a bit of luck, exhibited on the ever-growing LomoWorldWall.

The LomoWall

When we had our first exhibition in November 1992 in Vienna we were faced with an unsolvable dilemma: all our friends were heavily excited to present their Lomographs but somehow, everyone wanted to create their own space, size (huge prints, ack!) and format to exhibit their Lomographs. You know artists, with their airs and graces.

Beside the fact that such a presentation form didn't really conform to the democratic principles of Lomography, there was simply not enough space in our little depot to present all these pictures in that way. What to do? Without further ado we collected all our friends' negatives and printed them out once again all at the same size (at that time 7x10cm, the smallest and cheapest format available). Consequently we took a robust underlay, a family size package of glue and stuck all prints one by one on the newly created "LomoWall" together.

The result: a snapshot ensemble of Lomographs that indeed depict the democratic principles of Lomography. What was and is important is that the prints are multiplied and so repeatable patterns of Lomographs can be created. We call this the micro and the macro level of a LomoWall. When looked at from far, your retina processes the many different patterns of the LomoWall from an all-embracing perspective. Then, when you go close up, you recognise the many details, colours and shapes of each Lomograph and its associations.

The LomoWall remains the main exhibition form of Lomographs since its creation at the first Lomography Exhibition in 1992, and has ever since been applied from small personal walls in the flat-share toilet up to huge international exhibitions representing hundreds of thousands of pictures on mile long walls. We are deeply convinced that every Lomographer should personally enjoy the fun and satisfaction of assembling his/her own LomoWall.

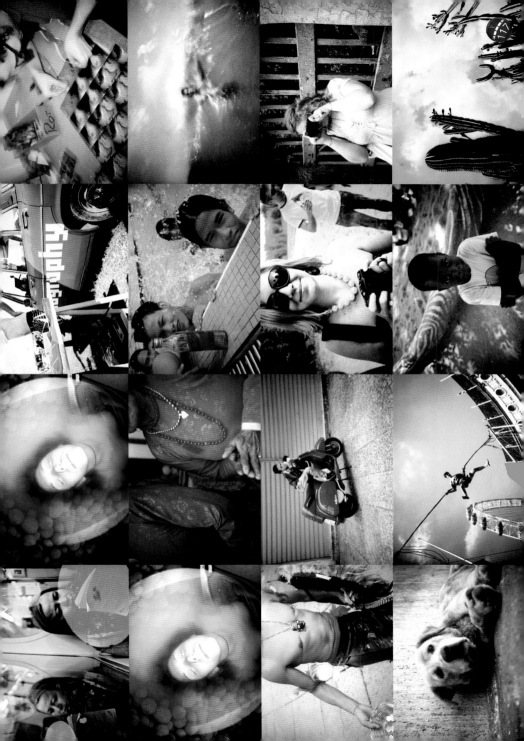

Lomographers are convivial folk and their regular meetings in some of the world's most beautiful places come as naturally to them as their Lomographing habit. Hundreds of Lomographers meet, share their images, life stories and ideas while getting to know each other, partying until the last roll of film is double-exposed and all the while, defining the state of the art in Lomography.

Major congresses have been held in Madrid (1997), Cologne (1998), New York (1999), Tokyo (2001), Vienna (2002), Beijing (2004) and London (2007). So where will the next congress be? We can't say anything yet. But you can be sure the next Lomography World Congress will present the biggest LomoWorldWall along with cutting edge challenges to sink your teeth into with a whole lot of activities that shouldn't be missed. The Lomographic addiction grows and grows and grows. Inform yourself on lomography.com and be sure to join us at the next congress!

The Lomography World Congress

Besides the many Lomography Projects, big and small, that take place worldwide, the Lomography World Congress is the largest official meeting for Lomographers from all corners of the planet. Our modest goal of the (nearly) annual Lomography World Congress is to unite Lomographers of the world, exhibit the current state of the LomoWorldWall and entertain ourselves in gregarious city challenges. These range from LomoTalks, which are very important debates about the present state of Lomography, analogue photography, society and the world in general, to other competitions of the most diverse kind.

And you,
How Are You Going to Take Part?

To connect with your new fellows you should first check with the **Lomography Embassy** (respectively Embassy or Gallery Store) near your town and see if there are Lomographic competitions, mini meets, events or parties going on in your area. There's usually always something cooking in the LomoKitchen and you should be ever vigilant so as not to miss out on an event. Then defiantly log on to the World Wide Web, register yourself on lomography.com and become active in the worldwide community. Uploading and sharing your images on our website is always a good idea because looking at so many different pictures can inspire others. Also, you will have a great time contributing to things such as the online **Magazine** (our interactive blog), the **Photos** section and **LomoLocations**; help us make the **LomoWorld Archive** (the compilation of all Lomographic pictures in the world) possible!

It is only with people like you that we can realise the creation of the **LomoWorldMap**. Then there is another option that we would heartily like to encourage you to do: make your own **LomoWall**. Hang this stylish ensemble of Lomographic images in your toilet or living room, in the national museum, the town hall or the Yokohama high-speed train. Why not? You should already know by now why the LomoWall is so important and why it is the ultimate form of exhibiting Lomographs.

There's nothing left to say here besides that the Lomo-WorldWall is also the heart of each **Lomography World Congress**. Remember, our goal is to take the first version of the LomoWorldMap to some place in the world very soon. Your images must take part in this visionary endeavour! Therefore, we would kindly urge you to join and meet up with everyone at the annual Lomography World Congress. As said, this is the biggest and highest official meeting for Lomographers worldwide. Every congress is vastly different and takes place in yet to be revealed locations somewhere on one of the five continents. Check back on lomography.com for all of our updates concerning the LomoWorldMap and the LomoWorldCongress.

ANYWAY, we don't care what you do and how you do things just as long as you're happily united with your camera day and night. Shoot tons of film and be satisfied with your results. That's just what we do and that's why there is Lomography.

So if you already own a camera, then you're a welcome member of our little association and know what to do. If not, then get a camera and join us in celebrating life and Lomography. Tschüss, dankeschön, spasibo, konichiwa, it's been a pleasure...

Your Lomographic Society

LOMO TIPSTER

Tips and tricks from the pros

There are endless possibilities of how to take photographs with the LOMO LC-A+. To give you some inspiration we have collected the 50 best tips and tricks from some of the most innovative Lomographers out there.

LOMO-STROBEFX

LomoTipster No.
submitted by sternstunde

02

page 195

DOUBLE
FUN

Lomo Tipster No.
submitted by ndroo

03
page 195

HOT DOGS

05
page 196

LomoTipster No.
submitted by lomomowlem

SLEEPY EYE OF THE
LOMO LC-A

07
page 196

LomoTipster No.
submitted by jeepeng

STAR
PICTURES

LomoTipster No.
submitted by danika

FROSTY DAY

LomoTipster No.
submitted by grad

page 196   09

D7 HAUTES CROIX

BONNE NUIT BAY

BRITISH ~~...~~

NO PARKING
FIELD IN USE

TOM YUM KOONG

FRIED RICE

NOODLES

SOUP or SALAD

STEAK

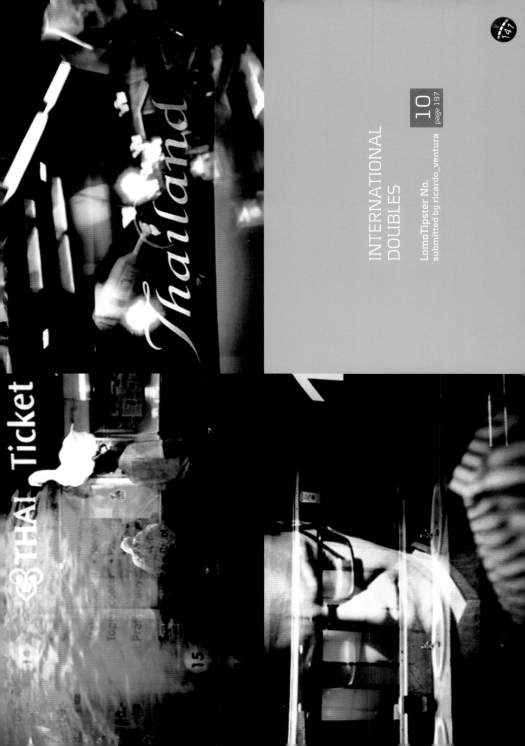

INTERNATIONAL
DOUBLES

LomoTipster No.
submitted by ricardo_ventura

10
page 197

FIRE EXIT

XPRO
MADNESS

LomoTipster No.
submitted by lolfox

11
page 197

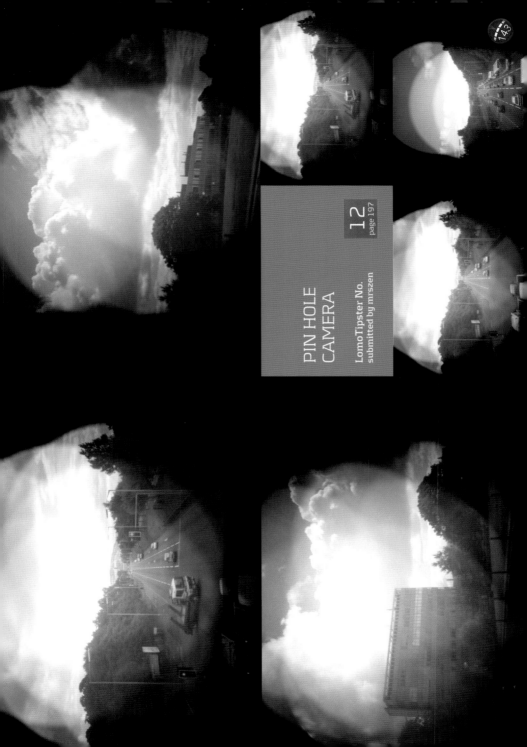

PIN HOLE CAMERA

Lomo Tipster No.
submitted by mrszen

12
page 197

BOD
MOBILE PHON
REPAIRS & A
BATTERIES
DANGER OF DEATH
telephone
096 9960
EDF ENERGY
HOT PIZZA
TO EAT HERE
OR
TAKE
TOUR 200

ENDLESS
MULTIPLE
EXPOSURES

LomoTipster No.
submitted by sandra_b

13
page 197

RIDE YOUR BIKE AND SHOOT...

14
page 197

LomoTipster No.
submitted by niccie

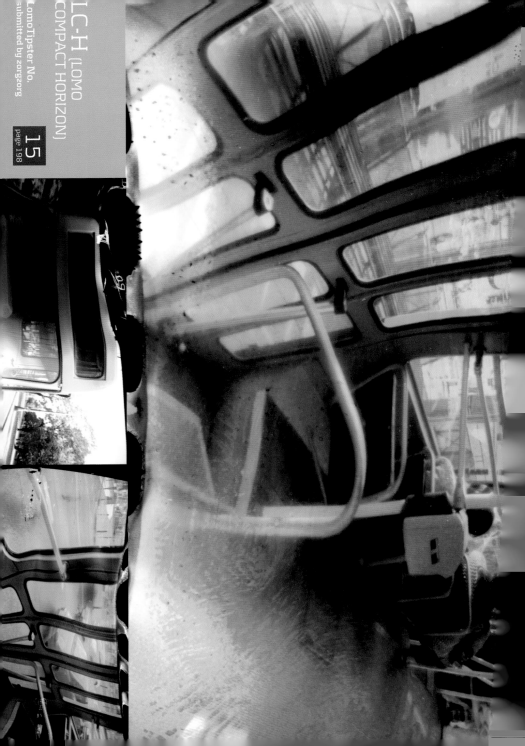

HEE-EE-HE

LomoTipster No.
submitted by zorgzorg

16
page 198

FIRST SHOT
OF THE ROLL

LomoTipster No.
submitted by mstrlss

17

page 198

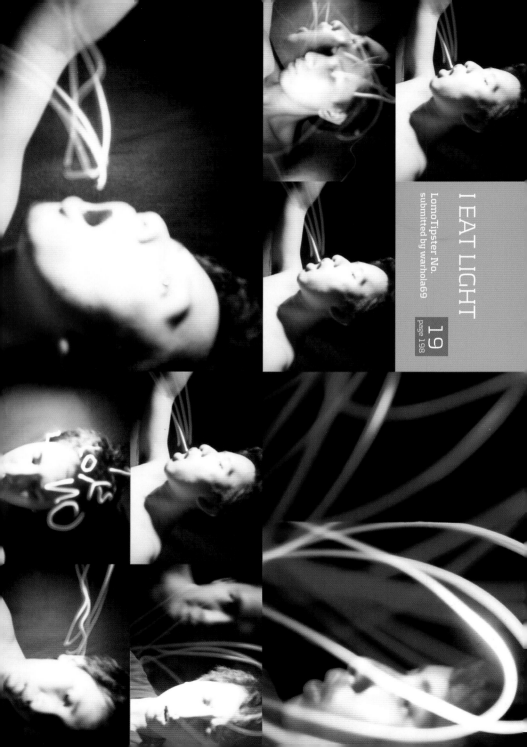

I EAT LIGHT

LomoTipster No.
submitted by warhola69

19
page 198

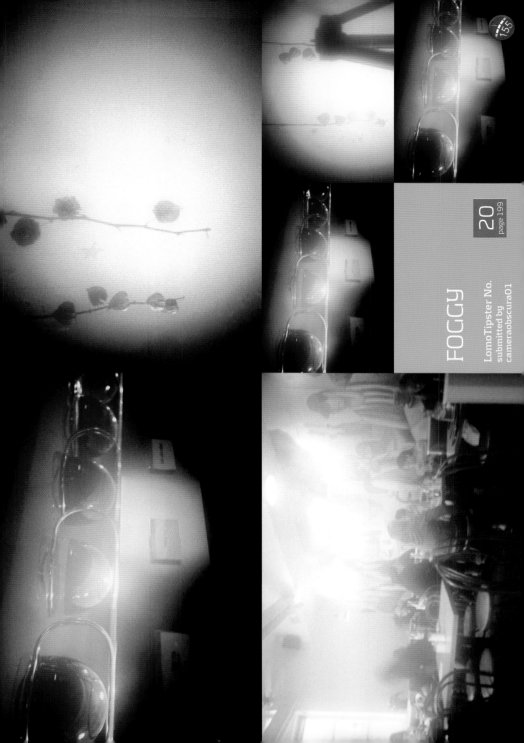

FOGGY

LomoTipster No.
submitted by
cameraobscura01

20
page 199

DEEP AND DARK

LomoTipster No.
submitted by noordart

21
page 199

FOAM
BOARDERS

LomoTipster No.
submitted by jonheslop

23
page 199

DOUBLE SPLITZERS

LomoTipster No.
submitted by
doubleswithvicuna and
grenoouille

24
page 199

PICTURE
WITHIN A
PICTURE

LomoTipster No.
submitted by illustr8a

25
page 200

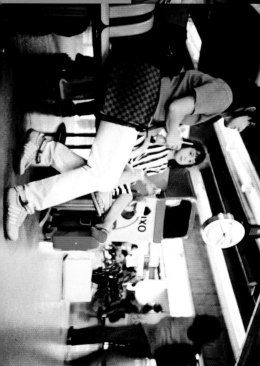

HOLD
POSITION

LomoTipster No.
submitted by minitar1

V. Mustafina

Lomo Tipster No.
submitted by zorgzorg

SHOOT THE
SHOOTERS

Lomo Tipster No.
submitted by luzian

28
page 200

GELS

29
page 200

LomoTipster No.
submitted by cmonkeyjump

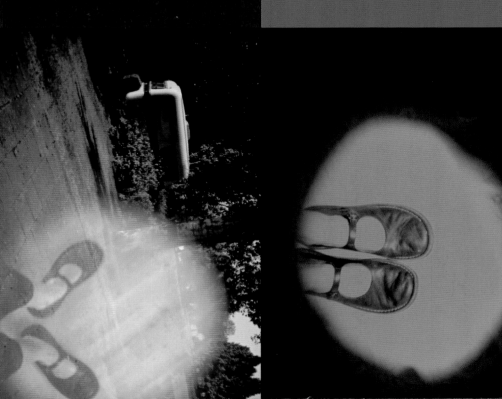

TOILETROLL

LomoTipster No.
submitted by
mireille_schoone

30
page 201

SPLIT FIELD
LOMO LC-A

31
page 201

LomoTipster No.
submitted by guderian_74

169

SILHOUETTE

LomoTipster No.
submitted by sammyhoi

32

STOP IT DOWN
DOUBLES

33
page 201

LomoTipster No.
submitted by pokari

IT'S A BIRD!
NO. THERE'S A
LOT OF BIRDS

LomoTipster No.
submitted by jibamz

34
page 201

NIGHT AND
DAY

LomoTipster No.
submitted by agrimony

35

page 202

WHEN NIGHT
FALLS... AND
DAY ENDS

LomoTipster No.
submitted by poshone

37
page 202

USE MX TO
CAPTION YOUR
PICS AS YOU GO!

LomoTipster No.
submitted by
angel-headed_hipster

38
page 202

LOMO LC-A
CHEST SHOT

39
page 202

LomoTipster No.
submitted by oulaifu

COLORSPLASH
FLASH
FILTERS

LomoTipster No.
submitted by
katya-leontyeva

40
page 202

LOOK UP AND
SHOOT!

LomoTipster No.
submitted by ragnarok

41
page 203

FOCUSING

LomoTipster No.
submitted by davanita

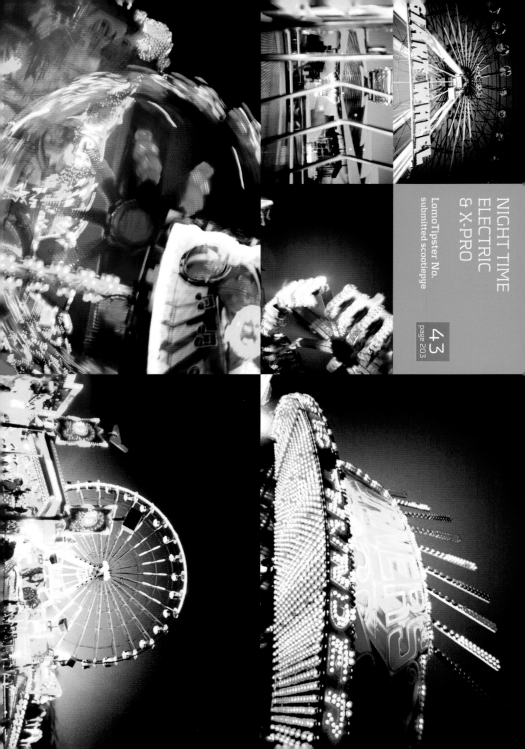

NIGHT TIME
ELECTRIC
& X-PRO

LomoTipster No.
submitted scootiepye

43
page 203

DON'T
ALWAYS
X-PRO!

LomoTipster No.
submitted by larslau

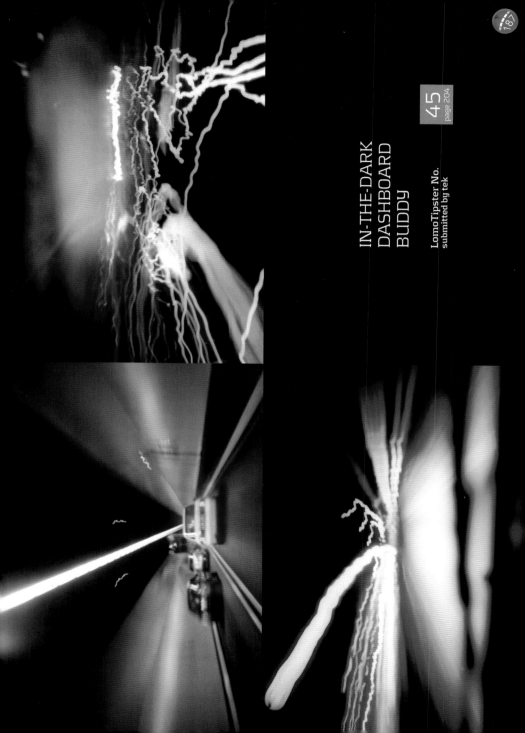

45
page 204

IN-THE-DARK
DASHBOARD
BUDDY

LomoTipster No.
submitted by tek

FISHY
LOMO LC-A

LomoTipster No.
submitted by reinertlee

46

page 204

PRETEND TO WORK
ON TYING YOUR
LACES AND SHOOT
FROM THE GROUND

47
page 204

LomoTipster No.
submitted by mephisto19

GET HIGH,
LOOK DOWN

LomoTipster No.
submitted by mistyfx

48
page 204

WINDOW

LomoTipster No.

49

page 204

submitted by roseability66

SHARP CLASSIC
IMAGES
POSSIBLE

LomoTipster No.
submitted by danielygo

50
page 205

LOMO TIPSTER INSIGHTS

Find out how these tips
and tricks work

>>

TRIPLE EXPOSURES
- submitted by ouroborosx

The LC-A is the perfect camera for creating multiple exposures as the manual ISO allows you to measure your exposures accurately, without overexposing your film. When you shoot double exposures, you merely cut your exposure in half by choosing the next highest ISO stop, so you can shoot twice on the same frame. Shoot 100 speed film at 200 ISO, 200 speed film at 400 ISO, 400 speed at 800 ISO, and so on. To get balanced triple exposures, simply go up 2 ISO stops. So shoot 100 speed film at 400 ISO, 200 at 800 ISO, and 400 at 1600 ISO.

One thing to remember when shooting multiple exposures is to avoid blowing out your first exposure with bright skies, because the second exposure will disappear. If you're at the beach and you shoot the sky first, and then a shot of your dog in the sand, you will likely only get the sky and your poor dog will disappear. But shoot your dog first and then follow with an exposure of the sky, and you'll see your dog with nice puffy clouds on him.

The LC-A+ gives you the option to shoot your multiple exposures right on the spot and compose your shots how you like them. But don't be afraid to try it the old-fashioned way! Shoot the whole roll from beginning to end, then rewind the film (listen for that tab popping out of the take-up spool so you don't rewind it all the way back into the canister), then reload and shoot again. Sometimes the randomness is what makes the magic happen!

02 LOMOSTROBEFX
page 126 - submitted by sternstunde

For this effect you will need the LOMO LC-A+ and the aid of an 'ActionsamplerFlash' to simulate a Strobeflash. The job of the ActionsamplerFlash is to burst the four flashes. If there happens to be a film inside the Actionsampler then that's fine; you will get a different perspective of what you have shot. It's nice. If you don't have film inside the camera, no problem: just open the Actionsampler and wind the inner spool until it stops as that way you'll fool the camera into activating the flashes when one release button is depressed. As with the LOMO LC-A, you just SHOOT! Remember to block the light meter so it won't stop during the first flash burst. Do this in the dark and try to make several flash bursts on the same frame… the more the better.

Attach different coloured gels to the flashes. It works great! Try to burst all the flashes while your objects move furiously, otherwise you will get all the flashes to burst all over each other and lose the strobe effect! Have fun.

03 DOUBLE FUN!
page 128 - submitted by ndroo

Randomly stick some unexposed film strips on your monitor/LCD. Open up an empty blank document full screen, and turn the brightness of your monitor/LCD to the max. Now take some images of the empty strips of film. Feel free to mess around with the layout of the film strips. Once you are done with the roll, rewind and re-load it for a 2nd exposure. Amaze yourself with cool and random results!

04 BOTTLED LIGHTNIN'!
page 130 - submitted by kylethefrench

Oh baby, just stay real still! Get a cable release and a tripod, and then slowly wave a fibre-optic toy all around you, or a friend, or family members – while you are facing a mirror, or they are someplace in the total dark (besides the toy) and then see the miracle of the LOMO LC-A long exposure.

05 HOT DOGS
page 132 - submitted by lomomowlem

Sunny Sunday afternoons are best for shooting dogs. Check out any park or green space and you'll have plenty of opportunities. To get closer, without freaking out owners, just go all soppy and act like their mutt is the most handsome beast you've ever seen – ask them if it's O.K. to take a pic and they'll almost beg you. And, of course, nothing beats a shot from down low.

06 GOOD QUALITY CLOSE-UPS
page 134 - submitted by seehorse

For good quality close-ups, I use glass lenses from magnifying glasses. Find focus from the sun, and set your camera's distance setting on infinity. The sharpness is just right immediately after this method of focusing: in this case, at about 20 cm.

06
page 134

07 SLEEPY EYE OF THE LOMO LC-A
page 135 - submitted by jeepeng

Want to see how the world looks when the lovely LOMO LC-A is sleepy? Point her eye on scenery or towards an object, half-press your shutter button (so that it won't yet release) hold on, and use your other hand to close half of the LOMO LC-A's eye, with the guard curtains. Now... SNAP IT!

08 STAR PICTURES
page 136 - submitted by danika

First of all, take a thick piece of paper and check that it fits inside your LOMO LC-A. After marking the right areas and cutting a star out of the sheet, place it in your camera – Go out on a sunny day and shoot. Then rewind the film. Now beware! You have to shoot again on the same roll, but at nighttime! Of course you can cut out other stuff as well, but stars are great!

09 FROSTY DAY
page 138 - submitted by grad

A frosty day creates unbelievably clear air. You should try it.

10 — INTERNATIONAL DOUBLES

page 140 - submitted by ricardo_ventura

Load your camera with slide film – Shoot the entire film, rewind it and send it to a friend on the other side of the world. You will get amazing pictures with a great mix of colours and cultures. If you use slide film and cross process it, the results will be even more amazing.

11 — XPRO MADNESS
page 142 - submitted by lolfox

I discovered this by mistake, but it's quite cool…! When I overexpose x-pro shots (I used Kodak Elitechrome 100 film) I seem to get crazy results by putting my finger over my light meter in daylight. Don't expose it for too long though, or else the whole thing comes out uniform reddish brown. I'm not sure if this is exactly how it works, but it's the only explanation I have for these weird shots that occasionally appear on my film. One tip is also to have a helpful lab that understands your taste for the weird: because many of them don't print pics like this, and just assume they are accidents.

12 — PIN HOLE CAMERA
page 143 - submitted by mrszen

Use a small piece of black card with several pin holes in it. Place it carefully in front of the lens and make even ordinary traffic look sweet!

13. ENDLESS MULTIPLE EXPOSURES
page 144 - submitted by sandra_b

When shooting multiple exposures, reload your exposed film at a different starting position each time – about a third of a frame difference is pretty good. To use the LC-A (+) MX switch instead, just wind the film on a little bit, after taking your pic – not a whole frame – then slide the switch and shoot. The exposures will blend and overlap, and then you can choose where to crop, or just leave them as long panoramas. Strong contrasts, shapes and textures help the exposures to bleed across the frames.

14 — RIDE YOUR BIKE AND SHOOT…
page 145 - submitted by niccie

It's easy… just be sure that you are good enough to ride hands-free because otherwise it could hurt a bit! Beware of traffic!

11 page 142

OK, as you can see, shoot a roll of film with your beloved LOMO LC-A, develop it as usual and give the negatives a STRETCH. Your LOMO LC-A suddenly becomes a LOMO LC-H. You do not need a panoramic camera then. Microwaving does not work... but you can use a toaster... or some other hot tool. Whatever you use, just make the negative hot without burning it, then stretch it manually and scan the negative. There you have your first panoramic LOMO LC-A images.

When taking pictures make sure to wear your mask! Take self-portraits and then shoot the rest of the film wearing the mask. My dad loved it.

16
page 149

When loading a roll of film into your LOMO LC-A don't be stingy. Wind on the film a little bit whilst having the back of the camera still open. You partially pre-expose the film which results in a orange-yellow-white strip on the first image of the roll. Embrace the beauty of imperfection and ask your lab to print the first shot, even if it's "spoiled ".

Take self-portraits with your LOMO LC-A.

Grab your LOMO LC-A, your flash and some penlight. Now: 1. Try to aim at your subject and click the shutter. 2. While the shutter is wide open, grab your penlight and draw something, whatever you like (just make sure the shutter is still open) 3. After drawing with the penlight, get your flash and fire away. Cover up the light meter of the LOMO LC-A for maximum exposure. Also try triple exposures.

FOGGY
- submitted by cameraobscura01

Breathe on the lens of your LOMO LC-A to fog it up a bit, then shoot. It gives a dreamy quality to the image, and the colours are messed up a bit.

21
page 156
DEEP AND DARK
- submitted by noordart

Use Kodak Elitechrome slide film to shoot a shadowy scene. And I do mean shadows, not the mere absence of light, but the real things that defy even the summer sun. Have the film cross-processed and you'll be amazed at how deep and dark the shadows will turn out.

22
page 158
SHOOTING FIREWORKS
- submitted by whimpee

If you plan to shoot fireworks, you have to take advantage of the features of the LOMO LC-A. One good thing about the camera is that you set the ISO rating manually, which gives you more control. When shooting fireworks you want to capture the light trails. Just set the ISO rating to the lowest level (100 ISO) while using higher film speed (400 or 800 are good). Because of this, the shutter stays open longer, letting your film capture more of the action. Good luck!

23
page 160
FOAM BOARDERS
- submitted by jonheslop

Here's an idea I had: 1. Find some foam and Blu-Tack. 2. Line matt black inner part of camera with Blu-Tack. 3. Stick thin foam strips onto the Blu-Tack. Use your imagination to decide how much you want it to affect your photos 4. Shake camera just to check all is stuck fast (unless you want bits to fall off, it may look cool, I haven't tried it!) 5. Shoot, shoot, shoot!

24
page 161
DOUBLE SPLITZERS
- submitted by doubleswithvicuna and grenoouille

As the LOMO LC-A+ is one of the best cameras to make doubles with, and as the splitzer is a fantastic little creative tool, grenoouille and I tried to make some splitzer doubles. We took 2 rolls – one was black & white, which we split to the left and right. The roll was a slide film to be cross-processed, which we split up and down. The results were really surprising, and resulted in fascinating doubles! So if you have a LOMO LC-A+ and a splitzer: make doubles with them and share your lomolove with others!

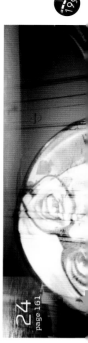

24
page 161

PICTURE WITHIN A PICTURE
- submitted by illustr8a

Use mirrors in your environment to capture a second view within your overall shot. You can capture yourself shooting the rest of the main image. Have fun with it!

HOLD POSITION
- submitted by minitar1

Just put your LOMO LC-A down on the ground, up on a shelf, or just let it lay on the table or chair. Whatever, just keep your toy on a firm support and click! Trying to get light strips by using a long exposure time, is a nice feature too!

SENSATIONAL CROSSING
- submitted by zorgzorg

If you want your pics to have nice warm red and black tones, take Fuji Sensia 100, and cross process the film. It doesn't matter whether you shoot outside or in, with or without flash — the images always result in deep red tones.

SHOOT THE SHOOTERS
- submitted by luzian

Take your LOMO when you are sightseeing with friends. They almost certainly have a camera, taking pictures every now and then. Just hold your hidden LOMO LC-A: ultra-ready to shoot them whenever they are shooting a picture themselves. Pretend to take pictures of whatever else and turn around just when they themselves are ready to shoot. This always brings interesting results, and sometimes you capture their object of interest in the background! An advanced alternative: shoot strangers while they are shooting pictures at tourist spots.

GELS
- submitted by cmonkeyjump

Don't have the colour-splash flash? But still want to achieve some amazing colours in a controlled environment? Try gels on your lights. You can pick up a cheap pack of acetate gels from most photo supply stores and cut and tape them to any light source. You don't have to use just one colour — mix and match! I shot these images with about 4 or 5 different gels on studio lights, in a darkened room... you can easily achieve similar effects to the colour splash, as well as cross-processing.

30 TOILETROLL
page 168 - submitted by mireille_schoone

I told you before you don't need any fancy things to create something amazing. If you don't have a Fisheye camera,
but like the round effect, just shoot through a toilet roll.

31 SPLIT FIELD LOMO LC-A
page 169 - submitted by guderian_74

This tip works in a different way than when you use the
LOMO LC-A+'s MX switch as it only exposes first one,
and then the other half of your frame. Take a strip of black
electrical tape and tape over one half of the lens. Shoot the
roll, and then wind it back for a second round. Just rewind
the film carefully until you hear the last part of the film roll
jump out of its fixing – you can insert the film again and use
it for a second exposure! Then remove the tape and tape it
to the other half of the lens. You get great images that just
blend together. You can shoot night and day in the same
frame. Remember to tape the viewfinder in the exact same
way each time on your reference point.

32 SILHOUETTE
page 170 - submitted by sammyhoi

Shoot into the sun with the subject in front.

33 STOP IT DOWN DOUBLES
page 172 - submitted by pokari

If you're taking double or triple exposures, and want to
get nice deep intense saturated colours AND a nice even
composition between the two/three expos, make sure your
expos are short and 'lite' – 'stop' your ISO setting 'down' to
the bigger numbers. If you're shooting with 100 ISO then
tune the camera setting to 400 during the day and 200 at
night. If you do this, then your exposures won't screen over
the top of each other and the colour will drip off the image.
It also helps to use slide-film and cross-process it.

34 IT'S A BIRD! NO. THERE'S A LOT OF BIRDS
page 174 - submitted by jibamz

Take a walk on a very sunny day, find a group of birds
on the ground or hanging on an electricity cable, run
towards them, and don't think – just 'shoot' them! The way
they fly is awesome. It's a credit to you if you're using Agfa
CT slide film, because your pics will turn blue!

31
page 169

35

page 175

NIGHT AND DAY
- submitted by agrimony

Put your splitzer on your LOMO LC-A+. Close the bottom part of your splitzer. Shoot one roll of film by daylight. Then rewind the film. Close the upper part of your splitzer. Shoot the film again at nicht. Your night and day shots are ready!

36
page 176

TAKE IT TO THE RAILWAY
- submitted by nicolomo

Bring your LOMO LC-A with you to the train station or subway next time. The lighting is always moody, but nothing your ol' Soviet chum can't handle. Also, don't forget to take the classic portrait with the moving train in the background!

37
page 177

WHEN NIGHT FALLS... AND DAY ENDS
- submitted by poshone

Start your night with the best colours nature has given. Thanks to the great lens your little precious camera has, the fading sky never was this beautiful! Get out, smoke your cig & wait until the sun starts hiding behind the clouds; capture the greatest colours ever seen in the sky above your home.

38
page 178

USE MX TO CAPTION YOUR PICS AS YOU GO!
- submitted by angel-headed_hipster

When taking multiple exposure pictures, look at the scene you are taking then look around for some 'writing' somehow related to your scene. Take the second of your multiple exposures of the available writing, adding an interesting caption over your image.

39
page 179

LOMO LC-A CHEST SHOT
- submitted by oulaifu

An alternative version of the classical hip shot is the chest shot. Hold your LOMO LC-A in front of you, turn it a little upward to make sure you get some amazing faces and then walk and shoot. People won't notice and the pictures are really nice, if you like faces.

40
page 180

COLORSPLASH FLASH FILTERS
- submitted by katya-leontyeva

Do you always lose those tiny coloured flash filters? Just stick the packet with double-sided scotch tape onto your colorsplash flash, and it will be much easier to hang onto them.

41 LOOK UP AND SHOOT!
- submitted by ragnarok

Don't forget to shoot what's above your head. It's really amazing what you can do!

42 FOCUSING
- submitted by davanita

For those like me with OCD (obsessive-compulsive disorder), blurred lomos are 'no-nos'. So to avoid blurred pictures, keep a visual reference of the length of the focus limits (i.e. 0.8 metres, 1.5 metres, 3 metres). 0.8 m is roughly equal to an arm's length, so for close-ups, stretch your arm out with your fingers touching your subject, and your viewfinder over your eye. Click! A perfectly focused picture!

42
page 183

43 NIGHT TIME ELECTRIC & X-PRO
- submitted by scootiepye

These shots were actually taken with the LOMO LC-A, using a 100 ISO speed AGFA RSX 2 slide film, and then the film was cross-processed. I dropped the ISO setting to 50 & 25 (which was only possible with the original LOMO LC-A) BUT, BUT, BUT, there are also ways to achieve these results with the LOMO LC-A+!

You could achieve this type of exposure shot by covering the light meter (at 2mm²)... maybe even for 3 seconds, again using a 100 ISO film. You would still get minimal blur with strong electric night-lights, but good strong images. If you want NO blur at all, use a tripod mount and cable release – but only if your hand is unsteady. Believe me, such images are possible by holding the camera by hand and simply covering and uncovering the light meter!

44 DON'T ALWAYS X-PRO!
- submitted by larslau

Combine the Minitar lens with a "vivid saturation" film such as Fuji Velvia or Kodak E100 VS, and process in E-6 chemicals (i.e. not cross-process). The result: some of the most amazing colours you'll ever see.

45
page 187

IN-THE-DARK DASHBOARD BUDDY
- submitted by tek

Some people have such a silly doggy on their dashboard, with its nodding head... and some have something much better! During an exciting night-time drive, just put your trusty LOMO LC-A down on the dashboard facing the road ahead, hold it tight, push the shutter and... wait! Hold it for as long as it wants to let those juicy nightlights streak onto its film. Afterwards you can enjoy your nighttime, 'road trip ambience' once more!

46
page 188

FISHY LOMO LC-A
- submitted by reinertlee

After you've finished a roll with your Fisheye camera, there will be a black corner in every single image. Use the same film again with your lovely LOMO LC-A and fill the black corners with whatever pattern you like. That means; combine the Fisheye with your LOMO LC-A! You can even double up with your companion or your buddies; you'll love what you have done!

page 189

PRETEND TO WORK ON TYING YOUR LACES AND SHOOT FROM THE GROUND
- submitted by mephisto19

Kneel down and pretend to tie your laces, scratch your foot, whatever, but SHOOT from the ground. Great for dog shots.

48
page 190

GET HIGH, LOOK DOWN
- submitted by mistyfx

Get to the highest vantage point you can find and do just what your high school counsellor taught you: aim low, way low... That wide miniature lens crams in all the beauty that most cameras crop out.

49
page 191

WINDOW
- submitted by roseability66

Shoot a photo out of your bedroom window every day, like Allen Ginsberg did... and see what the city looks like at each moment you capture an image. It's always different, and always the same.

50
page 192

SHARP CLASSIC IMAGES POSSIBLE - submitted by danielygo

You can use your LOMO LC-A to create wonderful, classic looking images that aren't necessarily the blurry shots usually associated with Lomography. Remember the LOMO LC-A was originally created as a "proper" point and shoot camera. Just compose carefully and then take a deep breath and press the shutter. Make sure you keep the horizon as straight as possible.

47
page 213

50
page 213

Log on to www.lomography.com and check out the user homes of the brave community members that submitted those neat tips and tricks!

www.lomography.com/homes

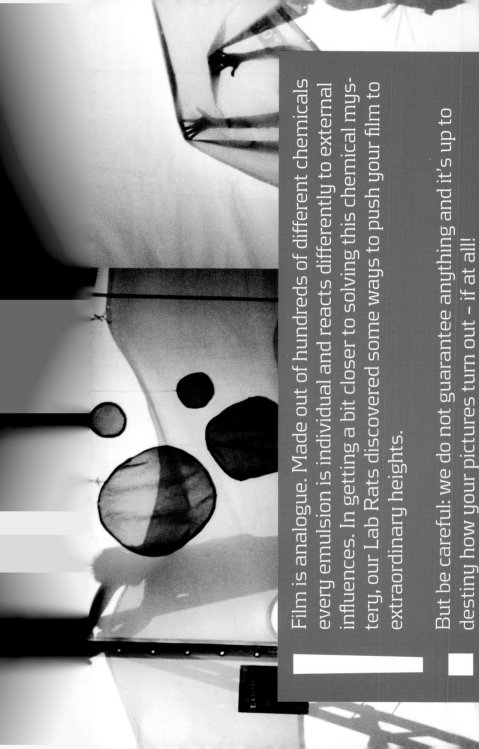

Film is analogue. Made out of hundreds of different chemicals every emulsion is individual and reacts differently to external influences. In getting a bit closer to solving this chemical mystery, our Lab Rats discovered some ways to push your film to extraordinary heights.

But be careful: we do not guarantee anything and it's up to destiny how your pictures turn out – if at all!

Cook'n'dry

submitted by mandi

The Risotto Effect: achieved by adding rice grains to a film, closing it up and leaving it to fester for many months. The whole thing literally came alive! The conditions inside were too wet to develop, so this is a scan of the negative. The effects you can see were made by mildew spores branching out and eating away at the emulsion.

Homebaked Film

submitted by mandi

This experiment does exactly what it sounds like! The best thing is that as long as the whole thing melts, you can develop this normally at your favourite lab.

1. Bake in the oven at 150 degrees or gas mark 3 for 10 minutes.

2. Leave to cool in the oven.

3. Develop as normal.

We used Agfa Precisa (cross-processed), it gave all the shots a slightly baked look, with a purple/blue tint and lots of grain. Other shots became greener rather than the usual orangey/brown.

Salt 'n' soak

submitted by mandi

An easy experiment that will add a little salt to your images, but won't leave a bad taste in your mouth!

You will need: a bowl, your developed negative, water, salt, a scanner

1. Mix salt & water. Ratio 1:3, 1:5 or even 1:10 for the brave and the bold

2. Put negative in this mixture

3. Leave to soak for a bit – a few minutes at least.

4. Take it out and let it dry

5. Scan it in – if you scan it in at a good resolution you can see the salt-crystals!

LAB RATS

Flaming Sambuca

submitted by wilber

Wilber said, "Expose the film to extreme colds, then instantly expose it to extreme heat. Or something like that. Bathe it in some flaming Sambuca?" Sambuca is clear liquor with a good amount of alcohol (3%) and a strong smell of aniseed. In Italy it is often served with 3 coffee beans floating in it (Sambuca con la mosca) representing health, wealth and happiness. A flaming Sambuca obviously sets a shot on fire.

Before we start, let's check if we have everything: Sambuca, a shot glass, negative, and a lighter (coffee beans are optical and optional). OK. Now we prepare the drink, put in the negative and set it on fire. What happens? The alcohol from the Sambuca starts burning. If you extinguish the fire after a few seconds, not much will happen to the negative. If you wait too long the negative starts burning, but just the part that sticks out. That's it!

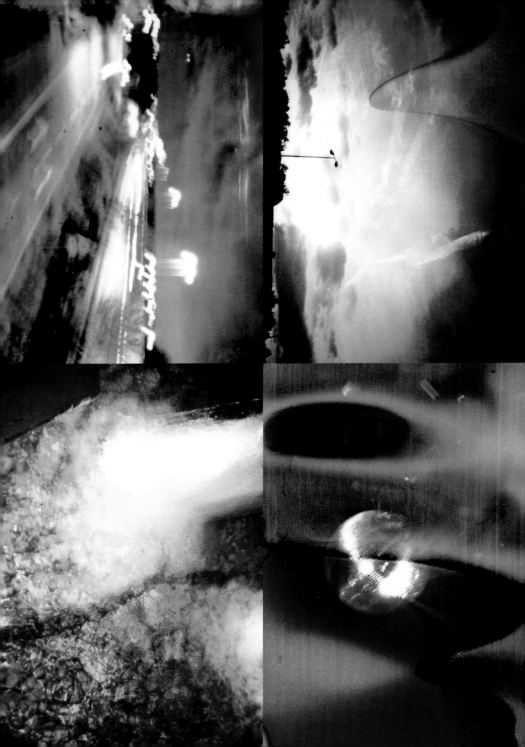

LAB RATS

Boiling Film

submitted by joncherry

Before taking photographs... boil your film in a big pot of boiling water. Gaffer tape your film up before hand. Or seal it completely somehow. Boil for 5-6 minutes. Put it in the camera and go out shooting. Also try boiling after photos have been taken. But just be aware most photo labs will tell you off, as the film will get condensation in it – so try to dry it out in a dark space.

Not Dirty Enough

submitted by Amstrad

I wanted more dirty grain in my pictures. After finishing the film, just drop it in a glass of water and salt. Then let it dry and develop it. It gets more lo-fi.

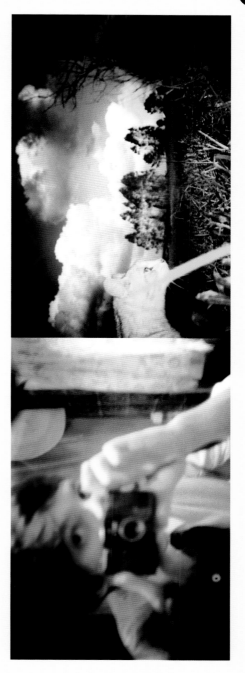

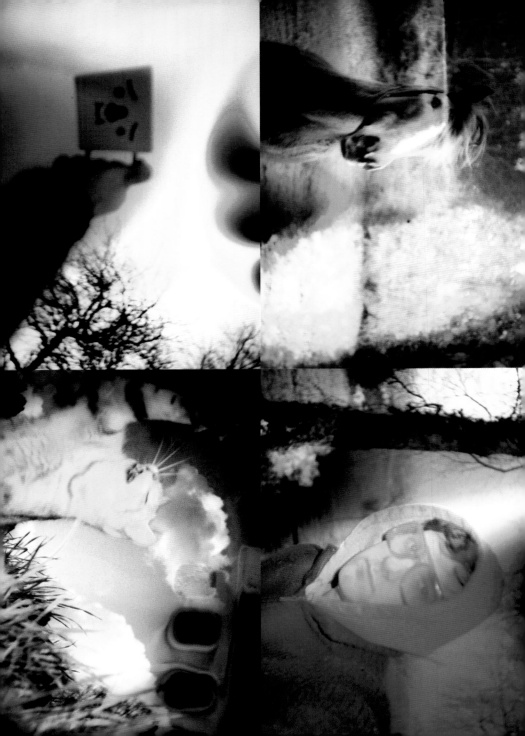

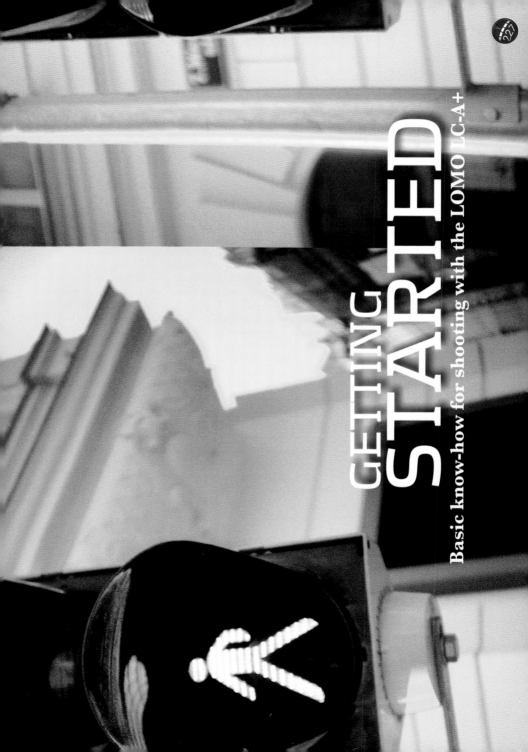

GETTING STARTED

Basic know-how for shooting with the LOMO LC-A+

Getting started.

Knowing the quintessential techniques and functions of your camera is fundamental to tapping into your full potential as a Lomographer. Here you'll see what the LOMO LC-A+ can do for you.

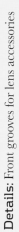

LC-A+ Tech Facts

Size: 4.25" (10.5cm) x 2.5" (6cm) x 1.6" (4cm)

Weight: 0.65lb (0.3kg)

Format: all 35mm film (colour negative, slide, b&w)

Lens: multicoated Minitar 1 32/2.8 ①

Available Apertures: 2.8, 4, 5.6, 8, 11, 16

Shutter Speeds: 1/500 sec to unlimited (via auto-exposure)

Exposure:
Program automatic (selects aperture & shutter automatically)
Multiple Exposure switch for unlimited shots on 1 frame ②

Flash:
Standard hotshoe with second-curtain synchronisation ④
Standard tripod & cable release thread ③ ⑤

Film ISO-capability: Up to ISO 800 & 1600 ⑥

Details: Front grooves for lens accessories

Automatic Exposure Setting

On the right, at the top of your LOMO LC-A+ is the light meter. It measures the light source and automatically selects the corresponding shutter speed and aperture combination. This makes sure that your images always get the right amount of exposure and gives you a lot of freedom to shoot and experiment with. In very bright conditions, the LOMO LC-A+ can fire off a shot at the speed of 1/500 of a second, whereas in low light scenes it leaves the lens open, exposing the film for up to 2 minutes or longer. All you have to do is go out and shoot...the camera does the rest for you. The little chip (light-meter) inside your LOMO is programmed with top-secret Russian codes, so you can be sure that everything will turn out well!

Whenever you're out there at night-time, you won't need a flash to get an amazing image. The LOMO LC-A+ automatically selects the necessary shutter speed and aperture required thereby allowing all the gorgeous ambient light to flow into the lens, forming an image with powerful, natural colour. Hold the camera still for a sharp shot (a tripod and cable release is the best combo) or move it around for abstract streaks n' blurs. Don't forget to switch to the appropriate ISO setting on your camera for perfect exposures to match your film speed.

Automatic Long Exposures

This is so important and amazing that we will repeat this point once again: at night, when there is little light, whether indoors or wherever else there is no sunshine: you don't need to use a flash with the LOMO LC-A+. The camera is programmed to measure the light conditions perfectly, and selects the right exposure time and aperture for you. All you have to do is press the release button (first "click"), hold your finger down and wait until you hear the second "click" – that is when the shutter has closed again and your picture is exposed on the film. When there is a lot of light (e.g: in full daylight) you may not even hear the second "click" because the shutter closes so fast.

However, when your only light-source is moonlight, you might have to wait one minute or so until the shutter closes and the picture is taken. In these kind of situations it's very advisable to use the cable release that comes with your LOMO LC-A+. By using it you are able to take a picture without directly touching the camera, which results in crystal clear and well exposed shots in low light situations. Of course you will need to place the camera on a tripod or a steady surface in order to obtain these kind of photographs.

The 'automatic program' function of your LOMO LC-A+ is so marvellous that it even works in 'real time'. That means that if you are taking a picture in a dark room and suddenly someone turns on the light the camera will react immediately and the shutter would close when enough light has been received for a proper exposure. The only thing you have to watch out for is keeping the camera steady to avoid blurry shots.

Holding the camera in your hands for a one to two second exposure is no problem. Just take a deep breath and keep your hands steady and you'll get a perfectly sharp shot. Alternatively however, a blurry image can be beautiful! The point is, you can take pictures, in any conditions, without needing a flash. You'll realize that your images will have that atmospheric and authentic touch you hardly get with a flash.

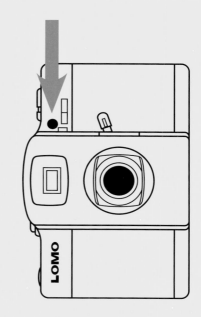

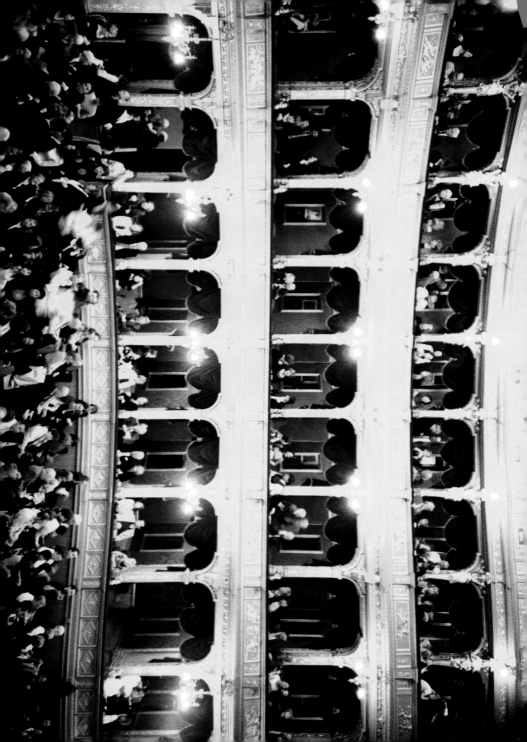

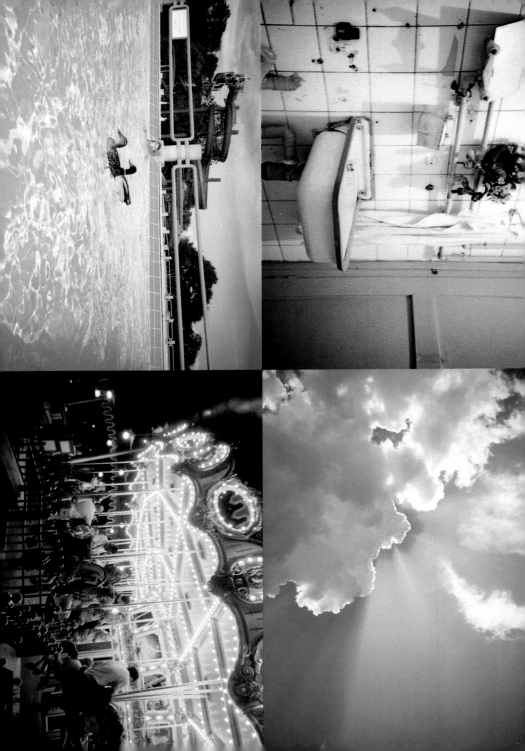

Check the Batteries

It's always good to check the batteries of your camera before inserting a new film. When there is no film inside, open the backdoor of the camera, point it towards the sky, cover the light meter with your finger and shoot a few snaps. You should see the shutter open for a few moments, then close. When the two red lights inside the viewfinder are glowing, everything is alright with your batteries and you can start shooting. If the shutter doesn't open and you can't even see one of the red lights, you should then exchange batteries.

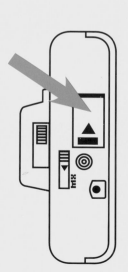

Flash Photography

Your LC-A+ has a little silver crown where a flash should happily slide. Once inserted, your camera will fire the flash whenever the shutter is fired – day or night. This point brings us now to the idea of the 'second curtain shutter.'

In practical terms, this allows you to bust out a dual effect image, where your subject is now a crisp and flash-lit little island swimming in a background sea of psychedelic lights. Just hold the shutter button down and let the camera do its thing – it will open the shutter first and fire the flash right before it closes. This is again due to our much beloved automatic exposure setting, which – irrespective of a flash being connected or not, keeps the camera's shutter open as long as the film receives enough light for a proper exposure. Just when it gets enough light the shutter will close before firing the flash. This results in an image where both the surrounding environment is captured (mostly background, unfocussed but atmospheric) and the subject in front of your lens becomes crispy sharp due to the flash. This function results in a glorious play of colours and is unique to the LOMO LC-A+! Also try taking the flash off the camera and firing it from a different direction while your little shutter-open interval lasts.

However, if you sometimes prefer a simple and clear-cut instant flash shot, just press and immediately release the shutter button, instead of waiting for the camera to do its own thing. The very pleasing result is a solid shot with nice dark vignetting at the edges and a shallow depth of field that only puts part of your subject into focus. When coupled with a coloured 'flash-burst', you can then have a monochromatic shot in the tint of your choice. To achieve this effect you'll need the Colorsplash Flash or the Ringflash.

Colorsplash Flash

The Colorsplash Flash sports a patented colour wheel system that puts several coloured flash filters at your finger tips for instant selection. The result: you dive your object into a burst of coloured light thereby adding an extra dimension to the existing shades of your environment. Insane images tinted in red, green, yellow, blue, pink and violet are the outcome!

Ringflash

The classic Ringflash was specially conceived for close-up shots, but with the Lomography Ringflash you'll add an extra layer of colours on top of it. Whenever you get really close to a subject; a normal flash will overexpose the image and – due to its position on top of the camera – not even light the whole scene. The circular flash element of the Ringflash, however, is mounted around the lens and allows for a totally even spread of light without directional shadows. Superb light portraits and close-up shots that make you jump for joy are the results! On top of that you have the choice of covering each of the four flash units in a different colour to really see your subject in a (in fact: four) different light(s).

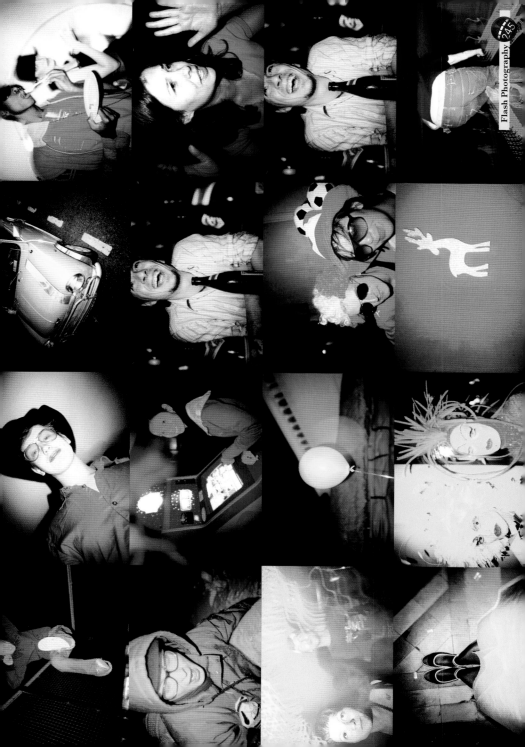

Use the Zone Focusing Feature for Shots from the Hip

The zone focusing ability is the most important feature for snap shooting. Instead of waiting indefinitely for the auto-focus or adjusting the complicated manual exposure of your camera, the LOMO LC-A+ allows you to adjust your required distance in a split second. Switch the lever to one of the four focus points (0.8m, 1.5m, 3m, or infinity) and shoot – you don't even have to look at the meter. It's so easy: use the top setting for close-ups and hold the camera about one arms length away from your subject, one down for subjects 1.5m away, the next stop down for subjects 3m away, and the bottom setting for infinity i.e. everything further than three metres away. Up, down, up, down, up, down. You're now ready for ultra-fast Lomographic missions and secret shots from the hip.

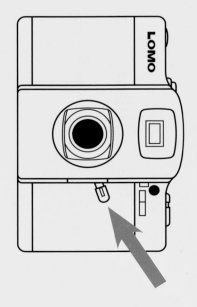

Cross-Processing

Any Lomographer worth his/her salt will tell you that cross-processing (developing slide film in negative chemicals) is the freaking bee's knees. It takes that sublime slide image that might-have-been and blows it out into a hyper-saturated, insanely contrasted, and wildly colour-shifted little jewel. The results are wonderfully unpredictable, and vary from film to film and from lab to lab. You quite literally never really know what you're gonna get.

Check out the Film and Development section on page 298 to get to know more about this technique, the right films to use and what to say to your lab to get the results you want.

MX-Button

A jazzy new feature innovated by and integrated into the LOMO LC-A+, is that after taking a photo, you need merely slide the MX switch to re-cock the shutter to fire off another shot on the same frame. You can do this a limitless amount of times. This is useful for day or night-time shots – and allows you to superimpose one image over the top of another. When you do this, don't forget to underexpose your shots: when you use an ISO 200 film, set the ISO setting of your camera to 400. Then your first shot will only be half-exposed, as will your second. Together they'll result in a well exposed image.

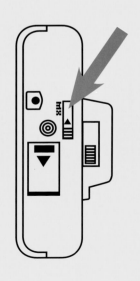

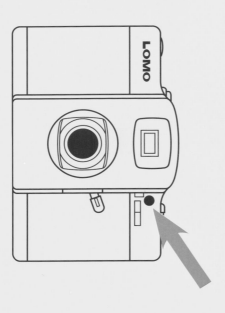

Use the Film ISO Function

The ISO capabilities of the LOMO LC-A+ reach up to
1600. ISO 100 films are slow and need a lot of light; therefore they are ideal for sunny daytime conditions, offering you
a finely detailed resolution bursting with colours. Alternatively, the ISO 1600 is perfect for low-light conditions, i.e.
indoors, giving your snap a grainy effect without additional
light. The range of ISO settings gives you bags of freedom
for over or underexposing (often recommended when you do
multiple exposures) your shots and are generally a great tool
for experimenting with different types of film and exposures.

LOMO LC-A+
Accessories

The LOMO LC-A+ allows you to experiment in various ways with the art of photography and analogue film. The attachments here let you access even more creative possibilities.

Wide Angle Lens

Affixed to your LOMO LC-A+ camera, this black beauty takes that comfortable 32mm view that we know, and expands it into a 20mm super-wide and full-frame paradise. Taking in 120 degrees of vision, your shot is still depicted as a full frame. The Wide Angle Lens is great for ultra-wide city views and landscapes. However, you can also go as close as 0.3m to your subject and still get a crystal clear shot.

Tunnelvision Lens

If you like the vignette effect of your LOMO LC-A you'll love this. With the help of a magnetic ring you can stick the Tunnelvision Lens in front of your camera's lens, thereby enhancing its vision with an extra wide-angle perspective. Unlike the Wide Angle Lens your image will not be fully framed but rather blurry at the edges, giving you that special Tunnelvision look.

Note: The Tunnelvision Lens was developed before the LOMO LC-A+ was released. It is therefore not fully compatible with the use of the Wide Angle Lens. You can't attach the Wide Angle Lens to your LOMO LC-A+ when the magnetic ring (needed for holding the Tunnelvision and Fisheye lenses) is attached to its body. So whenever you want to use the Wide Angle Lens, just take the ring off.

Fisheye Lens

This amazing lens gives your LOMO LC-A the ultimate Fisheye look. It expands the view of your camera to a range of 170mm; noses are stretched, lines are curved, and a nearly circular bubble frame fills the center of your otherwise rectangular image. The lens' multi-coated glass transmits clear light while cutting down on internal reflections – so the colour and contrast of the LOMO LC-A's Minitar 1 lens are preserved, ready to make you happy.

Note: The Fisheye adaptor was developed before the LOMO LC-A+ was released. It is therefore not fully compatible with the use of the Wide Angle Lens. You can't attach the Wide Angle Lens to your LOMO LC-A+ when the magnetic ring (needed for holding the Tunnelvision and Fisheye lenses) is attached to its body. So whenever you want to use the Wide Angle Lens, just take the ring off.

Instant Back+

With the LOMO LC-A Instant Back+ it is finally possible to translate LOMO LC-A goodness into an instant photograph. The classic vignette LOMO LC-A look, color-splashing, long and multiple exposures; plus all the camera's accessories, like the Wide Angle Lens, Fisheye Lens, Tunnelvision Lens and the Splitzer, are instantly accessible with the Instant Back+. Simply attach this accessory by clipping it on and press the release button to get your instant photo. Uses Fuji Instax Mini Film.

Splitzer

Attach this small piece of plastic in front of your LOMO LC-A+'s lens, and slice and dice your images as you wish. While you cover one half, one fourth, or more of your image on the first shot, you can expose the missing parts on the second by pressing the MX-button and shooting on the same frame. Thus you are able to construct absolutely insane images and mix up different motifs in the most prolific ways.

Krab

A reproduction of the rare 1980s' underwater case made by LOMO PLC in St Petersburg, the KRAB underwater case allows you to take your LOMO LC-A+ under water. By placing your camera in this case, you can dive as deep as 20m below the surface and shoot whatever you find. The KRAB is absolutely waterproof. Apart from underwater missions, it also fits your requirements for snowboarding on mountains or even landing on Mars!

Something you might want to know...

How the LOMO LC-A's Characteristic Vignette Is Created

The famous vignette of the LOMO LC-A's images was in fact seen as a flaw at the beginning of its production. The Russian engineers have tried to get rid of it for years, but thankfully never succeeded. See, because of the handy little size of the LOMO LC-A, the distance between the lens and the film can only be very small. As the Minitar 1 also has a very small objective, the angle of projection is bigger than it would be with a larger objective. Because of this large angle, the field of view that is projected onto the film is bigger than the actual film — the light naturally gets weaker on the edges and therefore produces the significant vignette on each image. Got it? Either way the LOMO LC-A's vignette is great and if our explanation for it leaves you dumbfounded then just take it as simply a Russian miracle to be thankful for!

How the Rich Colours Are Created

There are two main reasons why a lens like the Minitar 1 yields its supernatural saturated colours: **1.** The high quality and type of Russian glass originating from the sands of the Baltic Sea, known for their unique quality.

2. The complex coating of the lens which was specially developed for the Minitar 1. Due to the wicked construction and calculation of the lens by the Russian hi-tech elite, the Minitar 1 yields the rich and slightly oversaturated colours that we Lomographers love so much.

How the Lens Was Created

After the Minitar 1's calculations were finished at the world famous GOI-institute by Mr. Tarabukin (the 'tar' in Minitar stands for the first letters of his name) and Ms. Zhukova, they were transferred to LOMO PLC in order to produce the first prototype pieces. As the glass was expensive and difficult to manufacture, it wasn't suitable for a mass-produced camera like the LOMO LC-A+. It was the task of LOMO PLC's own Lev Sakin to improve the construction and make it suitable for fast production in 1984. Since then, the construction of the objective has not changed. Despite many rumours, Professor Radionov, based at the LITMO Institute, was not involved in the Minitar 1's creation; the only truth is that some calculations were made with a program that he and his team created for the Minsk-32 computers. Today the Minitar 1 lens is produced by twelve technicians at the original LOMO PLC workshop in St Petersburg, and is also reproduced in China.

FILM & DEVELOPMENT

Film and Development

Picking film for your camera is similar to choosing the right type of canvas, colours and brushes for a good three hours of painting. Even though the use of film and development is a bit more expensive than digital options, the wide variety and possibilities along with the simple flair of purely analogue film are definitely worth the price. A good knowledge of your film type (colour negative, B/W, slide film/x-pro) and film speed is already half-way to getting there

Colour Film

Nowadays colour film yields natural colours, contrast and wide exposure latitude, meaning that your prints can still look excellent even if your exposure is a bit under or over the mark. It's made of a simple sheet of plastic coated with at least three layers of light sensitive chemicals, which consist of silver salts. A tiny bit of pigment is added to the salts to make the material capable of capturing different tones.

There are a wide variety of colour negative films available, each of them offering slightly different colour tones and saturations — just try out a bunch of different brands and speeds to see which suits you best. There are films with 12, 24 and 36 exposures available. Even though the films with fewer exposures are of course cheaper to buy, they do not pay off in development. As you are paying a fixed cost for the film-development, the cost/performance ratio is certainly the best with 36-exposure film for fast-shooting Lomographers.

For all things film related you should definitely check out:
www.lomography.com/filmshop

Black And White Film

Shooting with B/W film is perfect for portraits and strong contrasts and gives your images a great feel. Developing black & white film yourself in a dark room also allows you more freedom and control over your prints. Black and white film is definitely the best medium for playing with light and dark, contrast and haze. There are also several variations on the market such as the XP2-film: it delivers perfect results and is, contrary to normal B/W films, developed with normal C-41 chemicals.

This means that it can be processed quickly and cheaply in any one-hour photo-lab, as opposed to the often expensive and time-consuming conventional black and white developments. In addition to that, XP2 film printed on paper results in Sepia-toned pictures, which can be a cool look. Sepia is an effect that is often applied in photography for its beautiful brown-grey tone. If you want to get this 'oldy worlds' look just shoot away on any XP2 B/W film and tell your lab to develop the pics in Sepia — any professional lab should be able to grant your wish.

If you are in search of ubernatural colours and crazy contrasts introduce your LOMO LC-A+ to slide film. Generally preferred by professionals for its better tone reproduction and one-step process (no printing, therefore less grain and more clarity), this type of colour positive film uses a different chemical solution than colour negative film. When cross-processed (x-processed or x-pro meaning that slide film is developed in C-41 chemicals instead of its usual E-6 chemicals) the colours become displaced and your photographs explode with brightness, saturation and contrast.

In practice, this means that you slam a slide-film into your LOMO LC-A+, shoot as normal and ask your lab technician nicely to cross-process the film. Each film and laboratory will produce different results. It is often recommended to even slightly overexpose your film and ask for no colour correction at the lab in order to get even stronger colours.

For more instructions on cross-processing check
www.lomography.com/x

each film has a certain date of expiration until when the manufacturer guarantees full functionality. Most professional photographers don't go for expired films, as the colour and saturation is not easily predictable – which is probably just what a Lomographer wants! However, recently expired films (expiration date of a year or less) that aren't really highspeed are a great deal because the results are often identical or very close to in-date film. Try out expired film if you want to add a little more unpredictability to your photo shoots and if you like to get a good amount of film for a bargain price.

Film Speed

When buying film, take care that the film speed matches the light conditions you plan to shoot in – a sunny day on snowy slopes, an event in a dimly lit room or a nicely nostalgic rainy autumn afternoon in a park.

Film speed is the measure informing you of the film's sensitivity to light. The most common film speeds are ISO 100, 200, 400, 800 and 1600. It is easy to remember – the smaller the number, the slower the film; the bigger the number, the faster the film. Slower films are less sensitive and generally need lighter, therefore longer exposure times. Faster films are fast in action and are good for snapping in poor light conditions although they deliver grainier and less colourful pictures. However, many people love the grainy, noir look that 1600 or 3200 black and white film yields. You should definitely try this out, as with the LOMO LC-A+ and a fast film you can shoot indoors without stabilizing the camera. If your film is expired, the film speed might change too – so you'd better be ready for some unexpected results.

You should never forget to set the ISO settings wheel of your LOMO LC-A+ to the ISO settings of the film you use to make sure that the camera's automatic exposure settings works properly.

You can also over or underexpose your shots on purpose: to underexpose a shot, set the ISO setting of your LOMO LC-A+ a few stops higher, such as ISO 800 setting for a 400 speed film. To overexpose your image, do the opposite; set the ISO setting to ISO 100 when using a 400 speed film.

Buying Film

Despite the rumours that analogue material and film will disappear slowly in our digital age, we can swear on the life of Lomography that film is still widely used by both professionals and amateurs and will be available as long as the LOMO LC-A+ exists (and vice-versa). Why? Because there are millions of amazing analogue photo cameras out there, because analogue film photography is becoming its own art form, because all big film companies have assured us that they will produce film forever and because film, in general, is not that hard to produce. Therefore, you'll always find all kinds of colour-negative, B&W and slide film in Lomography stores and on **lomography.com**.

Development

The choice between a professional laboratory and the supermarket on the corner is up to you. Whereas supermarket and drugstore development is definitely cheaper; labs offer you a wider variety of options regarding your prints and scans. They respond to individual requests such as asking for no colour correction with x-processed films (many supermarkets don't even offer cross-processing). If you're sure that you just shot a killer roll of film you might choose to pay a few bucks more for professional development; if you're not so sure about your latest experimental shoot perhaps you'd rather take the results to the cheaper supermarket.

The traditional Lomosize of prints is 7x10cm (2.8x3.9 inch) but as many stores don't offer this size any more, 9x13cm (3.5x5.1 inch) or 10x15cm (3.9x5.9 inch) are just as good. CDs are good friends of up-to-date photographers. Getting your images scanned on a CD makes uploading new images to your Lomohome a piece of cake. It is always good to order higher resolution scans; once in a while the Lomographic Society Rumbles kick off and you might find your entry published in a book. For 10x15cm (3.9x5.9 inch) prints the standard resolution is 1200x1800 pixels, but for bigger high-quality prints it's better to get a size like 2400x3600 (which is more expensive).

Scanning Your Negatives

In the long run, the cheapest option to deal with your pictures is to scan them yourself. Today you can get high quality scanners for a good price. These allow you to scan in your 35mm negatives yourself. It might take you a bit of time, but you'll also have more control over the results and the resolution. You only pay for film & development at the lab and therefore save a lot of money. A scanner is a good investment for any serious Lomographer.

CARE & REPAIR
FOR YOUR LOMO LC-A+

Care & Repair for your LOMO LC-A+

It might be handy to know something elementary about first aid for homo sapiens, but it's vital for a Lomographer to have crucial information about how to keep their beloved photographic tool ticking. In this chapter we provide you with simple explanations and tips to help you look after your camera properly and prevent simple mistakes.

Remember; any attempted repair is at your own risk and is not covered under the warranty.

How to Repair the LOMO LC-A/LC-A+

+ FRONT PANEL OF YOUR CAMERA HAS BECOME LOOSE

Have a look at the four tiny screws, two on the left and two on the right of the front panel, holding the cover in place [Photo 1]. Grab a small cross-headed screwdriver and fix the four little fellas back to where they belong. LomoDoctor recommends that once in a while, you inspect the condition of the screws to prevent damage or corrosion.

+ LENS COVER IS STUCK

Don't panic! Don't use brute force to push the cover open or closed. The best treatment in this case is to shift the front cover of the camera by removing the four screws on both sides of the panel. If the lens cover mechanism is not working or gets stuck, there could be a problem with the four flat silvery screws [Photo 2] holding the metal plate with the lens against the camera. While you've been vigorously snapping away the screws may have been shaken out from their holes and dropped into the shutter mechanism. Check that all the screws are in the correct place and tighten them carefully.

①

FOUR SCREWS THAT HOLD THE FRONT COVER OF THE CAMERA

Important! While fixing the screws, try not to scratch or damage any parts of the circuit board situated above the lens [Photo 3]. Any damage to the board could leave your camera permanently handicapped. Before fixing the front cover, turn it over and find the 2 small silvery knobs [Photo 4] on both sides of the lens window. These two should fit exactly into the small openings on the metal ring [Photo 5). To reposition the front cover, pull the lever of the lens cover to the right and keep the curtains of both the windows closed. Apply light pressure on the cover when putting it back. Test the opening mechanism by opening and closing the lens cover. If it doesn't work, keep cool and try again. If everything works, tighten the 4 small screws to support the front cover.

③

DON'T DAMAGE THE CIRCUIT BOARD ABOVE THE LENS

⑤

THE TWO SMALL SLOTS CONNECT THE METAL RING AROUND THE LENS TO THE SLIDE-CURTAINS OF THE CAMERA'S FRONT COVER

②

FOUR SCREWS THAT HOLD THE FRONT COVER OF THE CAMERA

④

TWO SILVERY KNOBS NEXT TO THE LOWER WINDOW CONNECT THE SLIDE-CURTAINS TO THE METAL RING SURROUNDING THE LENS

⑥

THE TRANSPORT MECHANISM OF THE LC-A (+)

⑦

PRESS THIS LEVER DOWN GENTLY TO MAKE THE
ADVANCE WHEEL WORK AGAIN

✛ LED LIGHTS IN THE VIEWFINDER DON'T WORK

There are many reasons why the LED lights cease to work: **1.** The batteries powering the lights are flat. Put in three fresh button batteries and test it. **2.** The metal prop of the +/- connection in the battery compartment doesn't connect with the batteries. Open the side cover of the compartment and see if the batteries fall out. If they do, the fault is caused by the small metal prop being pushed down and not supporting the batteries enough to get a connection. Take a pointed tool (a pen, knife or a screwdriver) to bend the prop slightly upwards. **3.** The +/- connection prop is corroded, stopping the batteries from having any contact with it. Take a knife or other sharp tool to gently scratch off the layer of corrosion. **4.** The two tiny metal straps situated directly under the shutter button don't have a connection with the advance mechanism. Attempting to fix this problem on your own is risky and doing so could mean your warranty is no longer valid. So, this time contact the LomoDoctor for assistance.

✛ ADVANCE WHEEL DOESN'T WORK – IT'S STUCK OR KEEPS ON TURNING

To exorcise the evil spirits controlling your camera's advance wheel, you need to open the bottom cover of the camera. Notice that the middle screw is longer than the two on the sides. Taking the cover away, pay attention to a small soft D-shaped piece sitting on the left (when holding the lens towards you) of the battery compartment. Don't lose it! It's small but very important, supporting the compartment's slide door from inside. On one edge of the bottom you'll see a complicated mechanism consisting of numerous levers and springs and a disc (Photo 6). This is the transport mechanism; a vital part of your camera responsible for re-cocking the shutter and connecting the spool to the advance wheel. The cause of the problem might be hidden here.

First of all, make sure that any of the small screws from the front cover supporting the lens or from the transport mechanism haven't fallen into the camera and stopped it from working properly. If not, move on and see if one of the levers of the transport mechanism is pressing up (Photo 7). Push it down gently and test the mechanism by winding the wheel.

Another cause of the advance wheel not working might be a winder with an oblong hole hanging loose. Put it over the small knob pointing up (Photo 8) thus connecting the transport mechanism with a bunch of springs. Test it by turning the advance wheel. If this advice hasn't helped, consult our LomoDoctor.

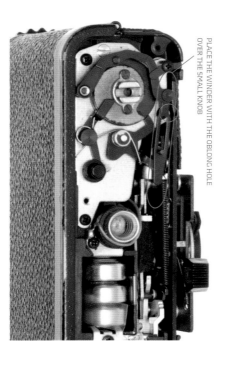

⑧ PLACE THE WINDER WITH THE OBLONG HOLE OVER THE SMALL KNOB

When putting the bottom cover back, make sure that the shutter is released so that the small MX button (multiple exposure button) can be connected with the levers underneath the cover. Also don't forget to return the small D-shaped piece back where it belongs, keep the slide door of the battery compartment open and make sure the D-shaped piece remains pressed against the main body of the camera (Photo 9). All the rest is a piece of cake!

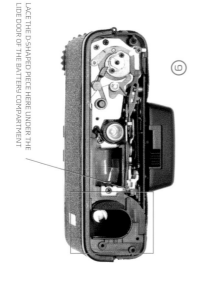

⑨ PLACE THE D-SHAPED PIECE HERE UNDER THE SLIDE DOOR OF THE BATTERY COMPARTMENT

No-Nos:

What You Should Never Do to Your Camera

✘ Don't carry your camera squashed between or under heavy objects i.e. books, laptop, your chihuahua, groceries or any other object that could damage it by compressing, scratching or moistening its surface

✘ Don't use any liquids or oil while repairing your camera

✘ Don't drop it into water, especially salty seawater, which will result in corrosion and rusting

✘ Be careful while disassembling your camera – don't lose any parts

✘ Don't touch the shutter mechanics – better contact a professional!

✘ Do not try to repair your LOMO LC-A+ when the camera is suffering from any of the following predicaments:

• Frame counter doesn't work
• Broken spool
• Broken hot-shoe

If any of these occur, contact the LomoDoctor: contact@lomography.com. Your LOMO LC-A+ can be saved and we will do our best to fix it!

Insider Tips from the LomoDoctor

+ Note that the middle screw on the bottom cover is longer than the other two.

+ Pay attention to the slight difference between the screws attaching the front cover and other parts of the camera.

+ Don't scratch or damage the circuit board hidden under the front cover right above the lens. It is a vital part of your camera!

+ To replace the front cover, pull the lever of the lens-cover to the right and keep the curtains of both the openings closed. Apply light pressure on the cover when putting it back. Test the opening mechanism by opening and closing the lens cover.

+ When putting the bottom cover back, put the soft D-shaped piece in its correct location to the left (when facing the lens) of the battery compartment. Hold the hatch-door covering the compartment vertically when replacing the cover. The soft piece should be left on the side and not under the edge of the hatch.

+ Don't cry if the small window of the frame counter is hanging loose. It can't escape anywhere inside the camera to cause further harm. If it annoys you, send your camera over to the LomoDoctor.

+ If you shoot a roll of film and all the pictures come out black, even though your battery is working (red light in the viewfinder is on), then it's most likely that the shutter is not opening. Test it by opening the back of your LOMO LC-A+ without film inside, and hold the camera towards a light source, for example the sky. Wind the advance wheel and press the release button – if you see the shutter opening for a moment, then everything is fine. If it doesn't open, even when the battery is working, then you need to contact the LomoDoctor.

THE HISTORY
OF THE LOMO LC-A+

The History of the LOMO LC-A+

Few cameras have travelled as far as the LOMO LC-A+. Invented by a Soviet optical plant rich in tradition, the tiny LOMO made its way from socialist Russia to Vienna where its discovery inspired a new art form called Lomography. It then hotfooted it into 21st century China, where it was resurrected and proceeded to conquer the world as probably the most successful snapshot camera of all time...

23.44 24A4

A₁

The LOMO LC-A from St Petersburg

The whole story starts in Russia around 100 years ago. In the year 1914, LOMO PLC, an optical factory based in St Petersburg, opens its gates and soon starts mass-producing the first photo cameras of the Soviet Union. Step by step our friends from St Petersburg further developed their cameras and were given their biggest camera-assignment ever in the early 1980s. The Vice-Minister of Defence of the Union, Mr. Igor Petrowitsch Kornitzky, spotted a tiny compact camera at a photo fair in Cologne and wanted a similar piece for each and every citizen of the communist part of the world. A few years later, in 1984, the LOMO LC-A first saw the light of day. The tiny black analogue snapshoot box was truly the first half-automatic camera of the Soviet Union. It was sold for the price of 75 Rubles all over the country. But even though the little LOMO had great features and was widely appreciated amongst communist comrades, the camera's future was uncertain. Political and economical circumstances were shaking Mother Russia.

The Berlin wall fell in 1989, the Soviet Union broke off soon thereafter and the newly found Russian Federation had more important troubles than a compact camera from St Petersburg. LOMO PLC concentrated on other fields of business and the production of the LOMO LC-A was going to stop. This was in 1994.

Meanwhile in Vienna...

But let's go 3 years back in time to Vienna, Austria. It was in the hot summer of 1991 when we, a group of flat-sharing literature, law, economy, architecture and so forth students were quite excited by what was going on just a few hundred kilometres to the East and decided to take a trip to the Czech Republic. After all, the borders to the former communist countries of the East were finally open; we obviously couldn't wait to see what was going on in our neighbouring countries.

Having arrived in Prague, we combed through the city and accidentally came across a tiny black camera that caught our attention. We actually didn't think that this so called 'LOMO LC-A' would be able to produce any decent pictures. However, we had somehow heard the name before from our good friend and well-known Austrian artist Heinz Czibulka, who, at a photography workshop, told us about a little nice soviet camera carrying the name 'LOMO'.

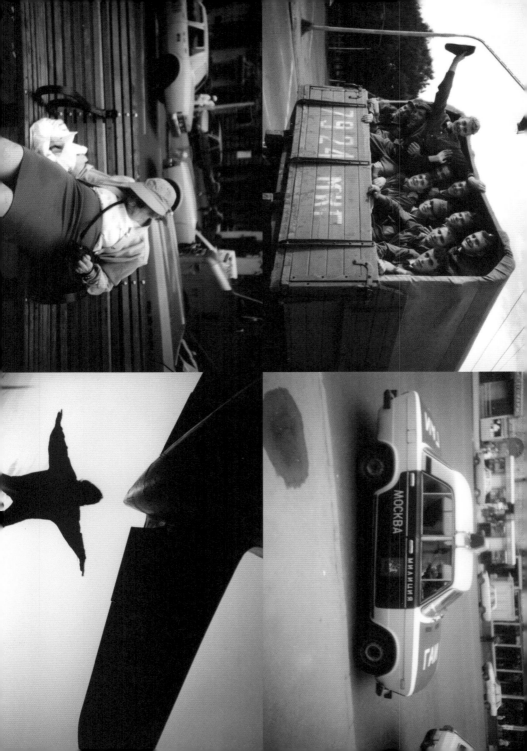

"WHAT THE HELL, LET'S BUY SOME OF THOSE STRANGE LOOKING MACHINES!"

"What the hell, let's buy some of those strange looking machines!" we sang in unison and dug a few korunas out of our pockets. Needless to say that the friendly look and compact size of the LOMO LC-A clearly attracted us. We then shot a few rolls of film, holding the camera between our legs, on top of our head, close to the nose and in other most impossible of possible situations. The tiny LOMO was so easy to handle that looking through the viewfinder was simply not necessary. Besides, what was supposed to come out of this camera anyway?

Back in Vienna we developed the films at the supermarket on the corner. Since supermarket chains had just recently started to offer and promote film development, it was suddenly about 4 times cheaper than before. Of course we chose 7x10cm prints — that was the smallest format available and was therefore supercheap! A few days later we got our films back and couldn't believe what we saw.

The result of our silly snapshot cavorting in Prague was a flood of authentic, colourful, crazy, off-the-wall and unfamiliar snapshots. From this moment on, everything went very quickly. Excited by this new way of taking photographs, all our friends wanted to join the newly-found group of LOMO LC-A lovers, get a camera and start shooting around.

We equipped the growing masses with LOMO LC-As that we imported in backpacks from Austria's neighbouring countries, baptized our little movement 'Lomography' and came up with the 10 golden rules out of the blue.

We then officially founded the **'First Lomographic Society International'** and organised our very first exhibition in Vienna at the so called 'LomoDepot'. This was a small exhibition space in the heart of Vienna's 7th district that the city had made available for us and where we organised many exhibitions and parties.

Incidentally the LomoWall was also invented in the LomoDepot. All of this happened in 1992.

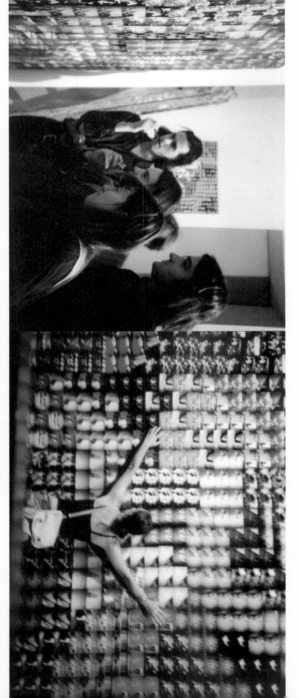

First Lomography Exhibition at the Lomo Depot, Vienna

One of the first LomoWalls ever

Our First International Exhibition in Moscow

Driven by our dream of sharing the gift of Lomography with the whole world, Lomography made its way to Russia and for the first time the USA in September 1994. Carrying the beautiful name 'Moscow-New York' we kicked off our very first international Lomography exhibition. We showed 10,000 Lomographs from Moscow in New York and 10,000 Lomographs from New York in Moscow. Simultaneously, the overall result of this insane event was shown in our good old LomoDepot in Vienna.

On the 31st September 1994 the first part of the exhibition was happily inaugurated at the Fotocenter in Moscow and one day later the New York opening in the HERE gallery in Soho (with the attendance and patronage of the prominent Austrian foreign minister Herr Alois Mock) followed. That was quite a big thing for us. Naturally we thought that we should actually invite the folks from LOMO PLC to join the event in Moscow. We had been shooting relentlessly for three years with the LOMO LC-A and had our first international exhibition in Moscow – who could be more welcome than the producers of the little gem?

However, at this point we hardly knew anything about the huge optical factory, and neither did we know that LOMO PLC were about to stop the complete production line of the LOMO LC-A exactly at this time. We simply thought that the LOMO PLC crew should see what colourful, authentic and crazy pictures their little camera was able to produce! Unfortunately we didn't get any reply to the fax we sent half a year before.

But then, just in the middle of the celebrative exhibition opening, Mr. Nikolay Mikhailovich Shustov popped through the doors of the Fotocenter. And so it followed that after a spontaneous speech and a few glasses of Vodka, the towering 6' 4" tall technical director invited us to St Petersburg. Hence, after flying to New York for our exhibition opening there, flying back to Moscow and taking the night train to St Petersburg, we found ourselves in the office of the general director of LOMO PLC. What a moment! First we explained what Lomography is and expressed our great devotion to the LOMO LC-A.

WE UNKNOWINGLY SENT OUR FAX TO ST PETERSBURG ON THE 1ST OF APRIL AND THE PAPER MADE THE ROUNDS AS AN APRIL FOOL'S JOKE.

However, the Russians hardly believed us. To tell the whole truth; we unknowingly sent our fax to St.Petersburg on the 1st of April and the paper made the rounds as an April Fool's joke. It was after all quite unbelievable for them that anyone still cared about the old LOMO from the early 80s. In the end we shook hands with the officials and took 300 cameras home.

When we left the huge factory building, the St Petersburg officials disclosed that they were going to stop production of the camera. You rightly assume that we were quite shocked. Ultimately we were in urgent need for LOMO LC-As to satisfy the ever increasing demand for the Soviet jewel – at this time we had almost depleted all Lomo-stocks of other former communist countries. This was in October 1994.

44,199

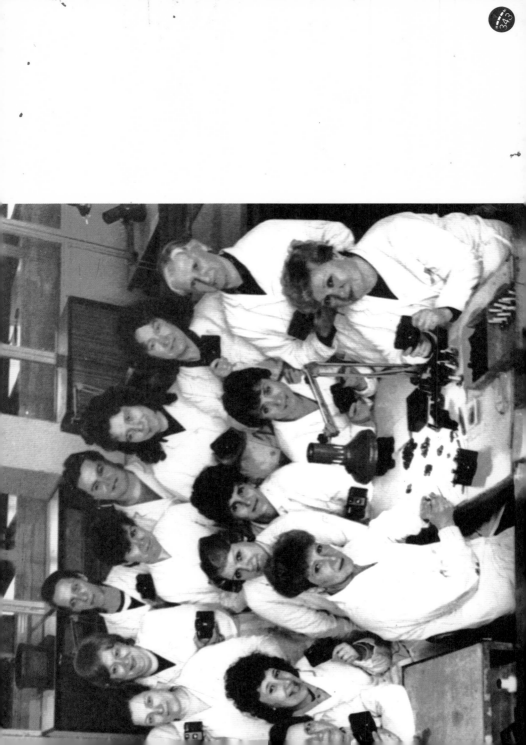

Tea-time with Vladimir Putin

Back home urgent life-related questions tantalized us. We had graduated from university and it was time for us to look for a respectable job and to focus on taking life seriously; Taking shots from the hip and promoting a middle-aged Soviet compact camera wouldn't cut the mustard, would it?

In any case, as soon as the Bavarian photo editor, Manfred, knocked on our door and subsequently wrote an article about Lomography in the reputable German 'Photo Magazin', the telephone, letterbox and newly bought fax machine of our flat share were on full throttle. From left to right and north to south it rang in our ears: "We want a LOMO LC-A!" New cameras were obviously quickly needed. But where should we get them from? In the West no one had ever seen the little Lomo, the shops of the East were long emptied and LOMO PLC gently disclosed to us that the production of the LOMO LC-A would end this year (1994). But alas, they were still the only ones who could save the future of our beloved camera! Hence, we sat down once again in a Tupolyev plane and flew to cold Russia. Our mission: to save the LOMO LC-A and the future of Lomography;

Our operations during this time included; having sleepless nights and wild parties in St Petersburg, meeting Vladimir Putin for tea, and finally, securing an agreement with our friends from LOMO PLC (Mr Klebanov, Mr Zalmanov and Mr Shmurov) that led to our mission being accomplished; The LOMO LC-A was back in production! At our meeting, we told Mr. Putin, at that time vice mayor of St Petersburg, about the great LOMO LC-A and subsequently he wanted to support our young business.

OUR MISSION: TO SAVE THE LOMO LC-A AND THE FUTURE OF LOMOGRAPHY.

A few weeks later he and the general director of LOMO PLC, Ilya Iosifovich Klebanov, made an agreement: soon enough our monthly delivery of cameras had resumed, arriving at our newly founded company in Austria. At this time we also got the exclusive distribution rights for the camera. It stands to reason that serious investments were made on our side in conjunction with this official deal and that our friendly Lomographic Society grew steadily. LOMO LC-As were sent all over the world and LomoEvents held wherever it was possible. We organised old-school group outings with new-style Lomographers (so called LomoTravels) to the most Lomographic venues of the Earth such as Vietnam, Paris, Havana, Moscow and Shanghai.

We organised the Lomography World Congress in Madrid, and we opened so called Lomographic Embassies in Bregenz, Munich, Berlin, London, New York, Tokyo, Havana, Paris and amongst others. Ultimately we began to develop and distribute new cameras, releasing the 4 lens Action Sampler in 1998 as the second 'Lomographic' camera after the LOMO LC-A. Many more cameras have followed since. And oh, we also launched our webpage in 1996. It is today the most important platform of Lomographers worldwide.

www.lomography.com

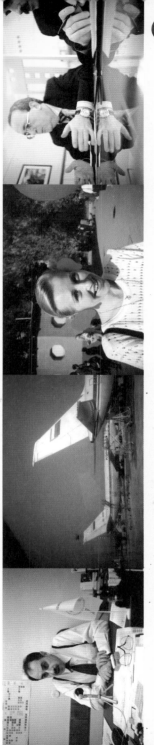

345

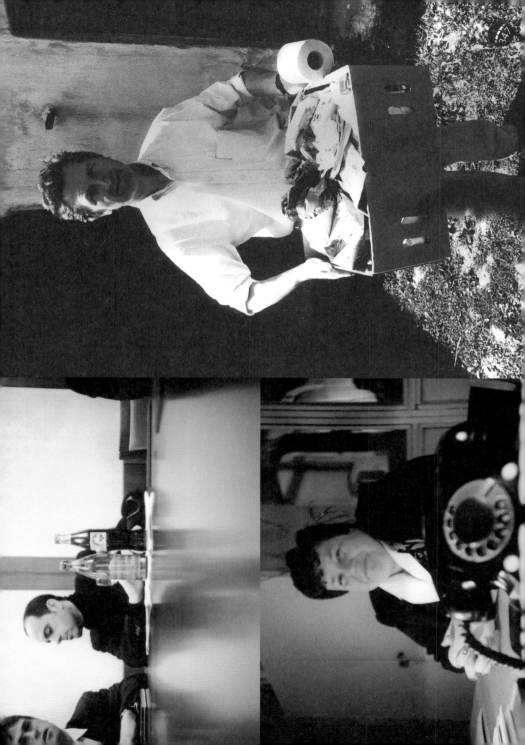

Lomography Around the World

What happened then? We kicked off more events, built more LomoWalls, introduced more Lomographic cameras (the SuperSampler, Oktomat, Pop9, Holga, Fisheye, Lomolitos, Frogeye, Colorsplash, Horizon, Diana+), published books, created our own photo accessories (flashes, lenses, clips) plus fashion, bags, stationary and film, opened up Lomography shops, developed our internet-base and so on. More and more people got to know Lomography and its different way of taking pictures, and to our joy more and more Lomographers joined our society daily!

However, despite all these merry events the LOMO LC-A had an uncertain future. It is necessary to remark that the economic circumstances in Russia had significantly changed since the change from socialism to capitalism in the early 90s. What had been produced happily before, through the help of a joyous minister, now hat to be calculated to the core. Throughout the years, LOMO LC-A's production costs (work, energy, rooms, material, capital) were constantly increasing, many workers with the necessary know-how retired and the production machines from the 1980s were not getting any younger either. The inevitable finally came in Spring 2005: LOMO PLC announced that production of the LOMO LC-A would be discontinued.

90°

The End of LOMO LC-A Production

Sadness filled our hearts and souls. How should it continue? Was it all finally over? Could more than 10 years of an intense relationship just go down the drain? Njet, njet, njet! Never ever! We would not want to let our good old LOMO LC-A down. Although we knew that it was impossible to continue producing the camera in St Petersburg, we thought that there must be another option. LOMO PLC themselves suggested that we go to China to find a factory to produce the camera. Even though the Russians couldn't continue to produce the LOMO LC-A, it was nevertheless the favourite of many senior officials of the company.

As unbelievable as it sounds, they were prepared to pass over all the plans and rights to the Lomographic Society so that the camera could be produced in China!

So we investigated the furthest corners of the Far East to find an optical factory which could take over production of the LOMO LC-A. However, whenever we knocked at a likely door, all we received was a friendly refusal. It was too complicated, expensive, risky, required too much capital – but honestly; who with any sense would invest in a copy of a 25 year old Russian analogue camera? All this took place at a time when no one wanted to believe in the future of analogue photography anymore and, above all, at a time when the Chinese economy boomed through the digital camera market.

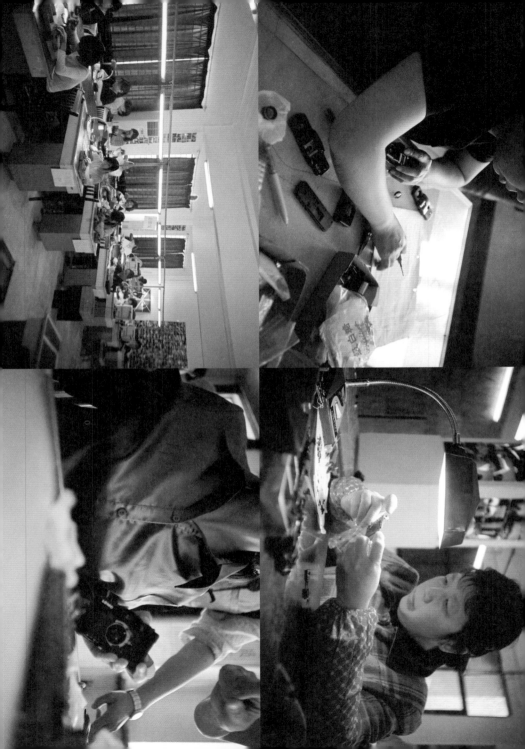

The Chinese LOMO LC-A+ is Born

However, we started an online survey on our website where every Lomographer all over the world was asked his/her opinion on the follow-up of the LOMO LC-A. The online community of Lomographers was an essential part of the Lomographic Society since its early days. We were keen to know what they were expecting from a new LOMO LC-A, and: hurray! The results of the survey truly filled us with euphoria: nearly everyone shared our love for analogue photography and just wanted the same LOMO LC-A pretty much as it was. Besides that, we received some important ideas concerning new functional possibilities for the LOMO LC-A. As a result of the online survey and the suggestions from our Lomography teams in Hong Kong, Tokyo, Seoul and New York, the first concept of the 2nd generation LOMO LC-A+ (say PLUS) was born.

We wanted to make a 1:1 copy of the LOMO LC-A, upgrade it with some useful improvements and features, and then produce it in China. Therefore the 'plus': the LOMO LC-A+ stands for the same feeling and charm of its original ancestor plus a few functionalities for the new generation of Lomography. Phew. Having all that in our brains though, we still had to find a factory that would accept our project. Thus we stumbled upon Colibri Manufacturers.

We found Colibri Manufacturers on a trip to mainland China in 2005. We already had a deal to purchase some cameras from a major optical factory in the Southeast of China but were still looking for someone who would be interested in making the LOMO LC-A+. When we met Mr. Li and his colleagues, we knew immediately that they would be just the right group of people for our bold project. For years Mr. Li and his friends gained experienced at one of China's major optical factories before they became independent with their own 'Colibri Manufacturers'. Knowing that these guys were excellent engineers, we presented our idea and to our great surprise got a "we'll see what we can do" in response.

A few weeks later, Mrs. Li (the chief engineer, not related in any way to Mr. Li) gave her O.K.: "Yes, we can produce the LOMO LC-A+!". Our Chinese friends were now working on the new and advanced LOMO LC-A. An active exchange between Austria and China followed, and the new facts and features of the camera were intensively tested and developed.

Made in Russia

Advanced options and extra functions surely have their merits, but one thing we absolutely wanted to be sure about was that the main characteristics of the LOMO LC-A remain the same. The camera's quick zone-focusing system (you simply switch one lever to adjust the distance setting), automatic long time exposure (even at night and if necessary — endlessly long), its charming "click" when taking a picture, the handy feeling and, foremost, the peculiar optics of its Minitar 1 lens absolutely had to remain unaltered. The vignettes, the oversaturated colours and the slight tunnel effect are, after all, essential characteristics of Lomography.

Ever since the LOMO LC-A existed, the Minitar 1 lens had also been produced in St Petersburg. To tell you the whole truth, it is the optical glass specially made out of sand from the Baltic Sea that makes the optics of LOMO PLC so excellent. By all means we still wanted to have the Minitar 1 lens produced in St Petersburg! And so we knocked once again on the doors of LOMO PLC in St Petersburg and proposed our idea of the 'heart transplant' to the Russians. Quite simply, the LOMO LC-A shall from now on be produced by Colibri Manufacturers in China, whereas its 'heart', the Minitar 1 lens, shall still be made in Russia.

We have to admit that even after more than 10 years of intensive study of the Russian mind, soul and humour, we had no clue what the response would be. Lo and behold; also from Russia came no "Njet", followed by quite an expensive but nevertheless tempting offer to continue producing the lens. "Da", for sure we accepted! Moreover, the Russians also sent a 20kg package with all original drawings of the LOMO LC-A from the 1980s to China. Obviously this genteel offer made production of the LOMO LC-A+ a lot easier.

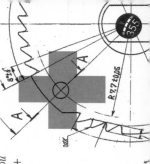

Releasing the LOMO
LC·A⁺

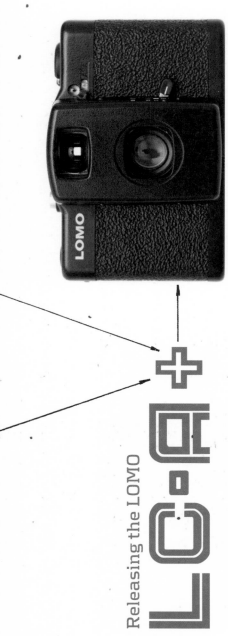

Everything was set, our nerves strained, our hands sweaty and our curious minds brimming with anticipation. Would the new LOMO LC-A+ really be just as good as the original? Can the Chinese do the job? Yes they can! In a record breaking 6 months after signing the contract, engineering began and in April 2006, the first new LOMO LC-A+ from China lay in our hands. And it even worked! However, this was only the first stage and further prototypes of the camera were then manufactured and sent to Vienna.

After another six months of the testing and pre-production phase the first LOMO LC-A+ cameras from China were presented to the world in September 2006, to be sold worldwide with their mass-produced transplanted hearts (the Minitar 1 Lens).

By the way, the Chinese have also been producing the Minitar 1 lens since June 2007. As the demand for the new LOMO LC-A+ was far bigger than expected, LOMO PLC couldn't come up with enough lenses for all the cameras being produced. We quickly asked Colibri to produce the Minitar 1 lens as well, and within the usual (superfast) amount of time, we held Chinese LOMO LC-A+ objectives in our hands. Nowadays you can choose between a Chinese LOMO LC-A+ with a Russian lens and a Chinese LOMO LC-A+ with a Chinese lens. Needless to say, the cleverly introduced Chinese copy of the Minitar 1 delivers 98% the same results as its Russian original.

New Functions of the LOMO LC-A+

So what's new to the LOMO LC-A+? Firstly, the camera has an MX button. By pressing this little button located on the underside of the camera, you can shoot more photos on the same frame and very easily create double and multiple exposures.

Secondly, it has a new little window displayed on the back of the camera showing the ISO-number of the film printed on the film canister. This is particularly practical for very active Lomographers as they always need to know what film they are actually shooting with and whether there even is a film inserted or not.

Thirdly, the camera has an additional ISO setting of 800 and 1600. This creates more possibilities and freedom to lomograph in bad light conditions, which the LOMO LC-A+ can now handle better.

Fourthly, the camera also has a cable release thread connection, which is very helpful for delicate long exposures.

And fifthly one of the simplest but most imaginative innovations of the LOMO LC-A+ is that small slots are added on either side of the lens. Via these 'Front Grooves' plenty of clever accessories (like the Splitzer and the Wideangle lens, see page 274) can be fitted, which extend the optics and possibilities of the camera. All of this creates the first true, analogue and evolving 'compact camera system' of the 21st Century!

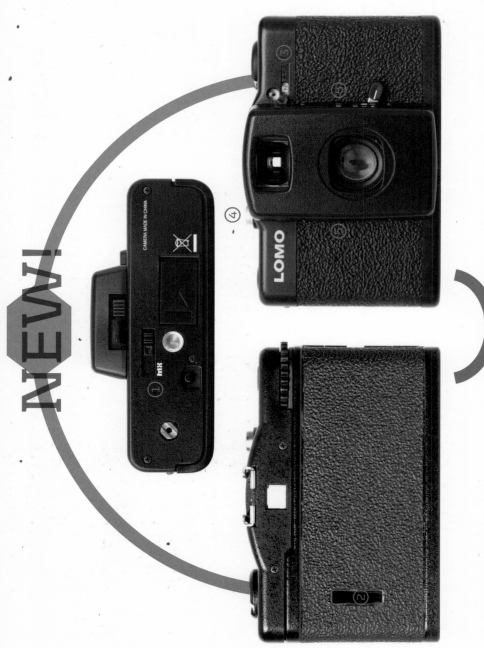

THE LOMO LC-A WILL LIVE ON AND OUR ADVENTURE WILL NEVER END.
THERE IS NO BETTER WAY TO SNAPSHOOT THE WORLD.

Lomo on!

What does the future of the LOMO LC-A hold? We're not giving anything away…. What's certain is that the LOMO LC-A will valiantly continue to have the main role in analogue snapshot photography. We Lomographers don't doubt that for a second! As long as there are enthusiastic, creative and wild lovers of photography who love the small thing and its extraordinary history just as we do, the LOMO LC-A will live on and our adventure will never end. There is no better way to snapshoot the world. Lomo on!

Well, that's the story behind the compact camera. It first began its journey in St Petersburg, continued in the unending vastness of the former Soviet Union, nearly became extinct, and then coincidentally found itself in our trouser pockets and hearts. At present, the compact camera is being reproduced by Chinese engineers according to the original Russian plans. However, we are not taking a break. Even though the LOMO LC-A+ has currently achieved pole position among analogue compact cameras in this century, we believe that analogue photography is definitely set to continue (and if anything, is only at the beginning) and will bring many new cameras, films, accessories and other surprises.

Timeline of the LOMO LC-A/LC-A+

1980: the Japanese Cosina CX-2, the official role model of the LOMO LC-A, is released

1982: the first complete working sample of the LOMO LC-A is finished in St Petersburg, Russia (then Soviet Union)

1984: the LOMO Kompakt Automat goes into mass-production and is introduced in the Soviet Union

1986: LOMO LC-As are given as gifts to the 5,000 delegates of the 27th Communist Congress in Moscow

1986: complete LOMO LC-A production moves to the newly constructed 'Filiale' halls in St Petersburg

1987: the LOMO LC-M, a planned follow-up model to the LOMO LC-A, is produced for a short time

1991: collapse of the USSR; consequently the demand for Russian cameras rapidly decreases

1991: a bunch of Austrian students 'discover' the LOMO LC-A in Prague, Czech Republic and so their passion for relentless shooting with it begins

1992: the first 'Lomographic Society International' is founded in Vienna, Austria, as a non-profit society to embrace snapshot photography with the recently discovered Russian camera

1994: all camera-production at LOMO PLC is stopped, including the LOMO LC-A in December

1995: 'Lomographische GmbH' (limited liability company) is founded in Vienna, Austria, to import and globally distribute the Russian LOMO LC-A

1995: the first exclusive worldwide sole distribution contract is signed between LOMO PLC and the Lomographic Society after future orders of the camera were guaranteed

1995: LOMO LC-A production is secured and restarts in St Petersburg

1996-2005: in 1996 the Lomographers meet Vladimir Putin, whose effort consequently achieves that LOMO-LC-A production is kept up. Following this meeting, many contracts are signed and conferences held between the Lomographic Society and the LOMO PLC officials to assure the continuous production of the LOMO-LC-A in St Petersburg

1995-now: Lomography Embassies, shops, travels, the Lomography World Congress, exhibitions, cooperations, interactive projects, web applications and other events are kicked off around the world

2005: Russian LOMO LC-A production ultimately ends

2005: Repair-workshop for used LOMO LC-As opens its doors in the building of the St'Petersburg Lomography Embassy, employing former LOMO PLC/ LC-A production unit engineers to refurbish used LOMO LC-As which are collected all over the former Soviet union

2005-now: 'Refurbished' LOMO LC-As are sold via the online-shop on lomography.com

2005: exclusive LOMO LC-A+ production contract is signed between the Chinese Colibri Manufacturers and the Lomographic Society International. Shortly after, LOMO PLC handed over 300 original technical drawings of the LOMO LC-A and Chinese production of the LOMO LC-A+ started

2006: the Made-in-China LOMO LC-A+, presenting new features and enhancements to the original LOMO LC-A, is released in September 2006

2007: the Splitzer and the Wide Angle Lens for the LOMO LC-A+ are released

2008: the KRAB, a reproduction of the original Soviet-era underwater case, takes the LOMO LC-A under the sea. The 664-page LOMO LC-A book is released

2009-now: the LOMO LC-A celebrates its 25th birthday and a special edition LOMO LC-A+ is released in its honour. More accessories, events, interactive applications and features are planned for the future

LOMOGRAPHY
PRODUCTS &
ACCESSORIES

Lomographic Products and Accessories

We constantly invent new tools to add to our range of Lomographic cameras, accessories and gadgets. Here is a selection of our premium products. For more news and detailed information on our products, please visit http://shop.lomography.com

Fisheye Submarine

Take the Fisheye 1 or Fisheye 2 up to 20m under the sea! Its crystal-clear polycarbonate lens opening means your shots are as sharp and bursting with colour as ever.

www.lomography.com/submarine

Diana F+

A faithful reproduction and a loving homage to the classic flash Diana camera – with all-new pinhole and endless panoramic functions. Includes the dazzling Diana+ electronic flash.

www.lomography.com/diana/products/diana-f-plus

Diana F+ Deluxe Kit

We are proud to present the ultimate Diana F+ package that comes complete with the full collection of Diana+ lenses, the 35mm back, Splitzer and Cable Release Adapter. Be prepared for all shooting possibilities and explore all the diversity of the Diana F+ with complete creative freedom.

www.lomography.com/diana/products/deluxe

Diana Fisheye 20mm Lens+

Shoot a 180° circular Fisheye image on a square print – bursting with the Diana+'s saturated colours and dreamy atmosphere.

www.lomography.com/diana/products/lenses/20mm-lens

Diana+ 35mm Back

An extremely handy interchangeable back that allows your Diana+ or Diana F+ to shoot four amazing image formats with everyday 35mm film.

www.lomography.com/diana/products/35mmback

LC-A Instant Back+

Wouldn't it be wonderful to have all the magnificent vignettes, colour-bursting effects of the LOMO LC-A camera, paired with its whole range of accessories - in an instant? Now it's possible, with the LOMO LC-A Instant Back+!

www.lomography.com/lca+/products/instant-back

LOMO LC-A+

The LOMO LC-A+ is simply the finest, most delightfully unexpected, robust, pocketable, vividly colorful, and soundly addictive snapshot camera of all time.

www.lomography.com/lca+

LC-A+ Krab

A faithful recreation and a slamming improvement on the super-rare Soviet 1980s LOMO LC-A underwater case – designed to take your LOMO LC-A+ up to 20m beneath the waves.

www.lomography.com/lomokrab

Colorsplash Flash

The famous colour-shooting, power-packed electronic flash. Soak your subjects with 13 different colours via the patented colour-wheel system.

www.lomography.com/colorsplashflash

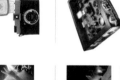

Lubitel 166+ Universal

The Lubitel+ is a loving recreation of the Soviet-era classic. Based on a design that dates back over 60 years, it's truly a mid-century masterpiece updated with stunning new features, including the ability to shoot BOTH medium format and 35mm film.

www.lomography.com/lubitel+

Fisheye Camera

The world's first 35mm camera with a built-in Fisheye lens! It sees a sweeping 170° view – compacting everything around you into a colourful circular image.

www.lomography.com/fisheyecamera

Fisheye No2

The new and improved 35mm Fisheye camera – complete with long exposure and multiple exposure settings, flash hotshoe, Fisheye viewfinder, and "full metal jacket" body treatment.

www.lomography.com/fisheye

Diana+ Instant Back

Instant photography lives on with the Diana+ Instant Back. This attachment to any Diana+ or DianaF+ camera uses readily available and freshly produced Fuji Instax Mini film to create instantaneous credit card sized images. Add any of the Diana+ lenses for truly unique instant Lomography.

www.lomography.com/diana/products/instant

Diana Mini

Never before has something so little given so much on 35mm film! Square or rectangular 'half frame' frame modes, multiple and overlapped exposures, flash, long night-time exposures and much more with the Diana Mini!

www.lomography.com/dianamini

Supersampler

This Queen of all Multi-Lensed Cameras shoots four panoramic images on one standard print with just a pull of the ripcord.

www.lomography.com/supersampler

Colorsplash Camera

Soak your subjects in a burst of beautiful coloured light with the patented colour-wheel system. Use the long-exposure function for blurry backgrounds and sharp Colorsplashed foregrounds.

www.lomography.com/colorsplashcamera

Chakra Edition Colorsplash Camera

This sleek Lomographic Colorsplashing machine has been customised by NYC's Staple Design as an exclusive limited edition.

www.lomography.com/colorsplashchakra

Actionsampler

The original photo-photo-photo-photo camera. One touch of the shutter equals four images on one print.

www.lomography.com/actionsampler

Actionsampler Chrome

The Actionsampler clad in a sexy chrome coat.

Actionsampler Flash

Enough of early bedtimes, your Actionsampling night fever is here. Using the same beloved 4-shot format of our classic Actionsampler, the Actionsampler Flash tosses in an additional 4-step sequential flash.

www.lomography.com/actionsampler

Oktomat

SHOOT!! And 8 "clacks" later your subject is cleanly sliced into 8 little frames, boiled, and served. The action takes place over 2 seconds.

www.lomography.com/oktomat

Pop 9

One single shot produces 9 identical images on one print – instantaneously transforming the environment around you into explosions of pattern-repeating pop-art.

www.lomography.com/pop9

Horizon Kompakt

The easy-going snapshot panoramic camera. With a fixed aperture and focus, all you have to do is aim... point, and shoot! Crafted in Russia, its incredible swing-lens sweeps across and sees a full 120° angle.

www.lomography.com/horizon/kompakt

Horizon Perfekt

The professional panoramic choice. Crafted in Russia, its incredible swing-lens sweeps across and sees a full 120° angle.
www.lomography.com/horizon/perfekt

Lomolitos

A true revolution in Lomography - the first single-use Lomographic camera! Each camera includes a single colour filter that can be switched on or off your flash.
www.lomography.com/lomolitos

Ringflash

When mounted onto your camera, the Ringflash completely surrounds your lens and throws a burst of perfectly even white or coloured flash light onto your subject – making for fantastic close-up portraits with a signature look.
www.lomography.com/ringflash

Fotoclips

Introducing two new dimensions to photography. Every bag contains clear 2D and orange 3D Fotoclips, empowering you to create unlimited constructions of your own beautiful Lomographs!
www.lomography.com/fotoclips

Fisheye Circle Cutter

You are hereby liberated from the gulag of square shapes and right angles: your most precious Lomographic prints can now be beautiful, curvy circles with just a twist of your hand.
www.lomography.com/circlecutter

Tazzas

The Lomography Tazza cups bring style and grace to your morning coffee or your afternoon tea. Enjoy a cappuccino in the Tazza Grande cups or an espresso in the Tazza Piccola cup. Each cup features a drawing by Russian artist Alexander Djkia.
shop.lomography.com

Sushi Tea Cup

Pour some Lomography love into your cup. Now you can enjoy your drink and proclaim your analogue love at the same time! Your favorite Lomography cameras are creatively illustrated all over this special Lomography Sushi Cup.
shop.lomography.com

Shutter Buttons

Wear your Lomographic Badge of Love and Pride with these snazzy Lomography Shutter Buttons! These circular snapshots of Lomography come in various designs that will compliment your already-smashing sense of style. Pin it on your shirt, bag, or necktie – to add a dose of analogue coolness to your wardrobe!
shop.lomography.com

Womens Tank Tops

Each LomoGRAPHIC t-shirt is hand crafted in extremely soft 100% organic Egyptian cotton, and emblazoned with a bold and durable screen print (done with environmentally friendly ink, of course). Available in both men's and women's patterns – with a variety of colours and motifs.
www.lomography.com/fashion

Mens Crewneck T-Shirt

Our textile products are made from organic cotton, and the products are ISO 9001 certified and fully conform to the international Demeter guidelines! Made in Egypt by highly qualified craftsmen!
www.lomography.com/fashion

Sidekick Bag TPE

A companion for all of your adventures, the unisex Sidekick bag holds your precious Lomographic cameras at easy reach while easily toting all of your daily wares. Available in two sizes (large & small) and several attractive colourways.

www.lomography.com/sidekick

Sidekick Bag Leather

Take your cameras everywhere you go! Made in Egypt with the finest pebble-grain leather, the Sidekick leather bag features a 2-in-1 design – a small bag to store your valued cameras and a large bag that holds a laptop and other documents in place.

www.lomography.com/sidekick

Lomofolio Bag

Whatever mood you're in, whatever style you swing – the Lomofolio is the everyday fashionista bag that fits right in. Made from the most exquisitely soft Nappa leather, every detail has functionality and style in mind.

www.lomography.com/lomofolio

Lomography Packrat Bag

An easy carry-all for your daily comings and goings – crafted in durable cotton canvas. Day in, day out, this faithful tote is by your side and ready to transport your most necessary essentials. Available in large and X-large sizes.

www.lomography.com/packratbag

LOMO LC-A Book

This is the full, unabridged LOMO LC-A Book. Two years in the making with the help of thousands of images submitted by the Lomographic community, this book encapsulates over 25 years of LC-A history. Stuffed with more than 3,000 unique images shot with this unmistakable camera hailing from St Petersburg, the book traces the LOMO LC-A back to its roots.

www.lomography.com/lcabook

Lubitel+ Book

"Love from Waist Level" presents a full-bodied look at the grand past and absolutely brilliant future of the original Lubitel and Lubitel+ cameras. Bound in hardback, this colourful edition is packed shut with expert interviews, historical tales and images, Lubitel Lover profiles, inspirational tips and tricks, and an enormous gallery of mind-blowing medium format and 35mm Lubitel images!

www.lomography.com/lubitelbook

Colorsplash Chakras Book

Designed by Staple and published by Lomography, this 384-page hardback edition details the philosophy and story of the Colorsplash Chakra project.

www.lomography.com/colorsplashchakra

Fisheye Book

This definitive compendium of all things Fisheye features exclusive tips and tricks, Lomographer profiles and interviews, and several hundred eye-popping barrel-distorted Fisheye images of every type.

www.lomography.com/fisheye

Don't Think * Just Shoot

Don't Think * Just Shoot broke new ground by evolving into a visual time line of life and experience from all corners of the globe. You can find 2,000 vibrant, analogue LC-A submissions inside.

www.lomography.com/lca+

Lomography Keychains

Your favourite Lomographic cameras – Lubitel+, Diana F+, Fisheye 2, and the LOMO LC-A+ have been turned into miniature keychains! Add a nice touch to your style, by using them as mobile phone/camera charms, or as a cute add-on to your outfit!

shop.lomography.com